A BRIEF HISTORY OF SHELBY COUNTY

INDIANA

JULIE YOUNG

THE History PRESS

Published by The History Press
Charleston, SC 29403
www.historypress.net

All images courtesy of John Rouse with the Shelby County Alumni Association unless otherwise noted.

First published 2010

Manufactured in the United States
ISBN 978.1.59629.846.0
Library of Congress Cataloging-in-Publication Data
Young, Julie.
a brief history of Shelby County, Indiana / Julie Young.
p. cm.
Includes bibliographical references.
ISBN 978-1-59629-846-0
1. Shelby County (Ind.)--History, Local. I. Title.
F532.S5Y68 2010
977.2'59--dc22
2009053680

To my great-uncle, the late Sherman Williams, with love.

CONTENTS

Acknowledgements 7
Introduction 9

1. Opening the Wilderness 13
2. Shelbyville: Pride in Progress 21
3. Transactions and Transportation 47
4. Jacket Country 59
5. The Camp Atterbury Connection 87
6. Fairland and Boggstown 91
7. Unincorporated Communities 101
8. Famous Shelby County Residents 121
9. Shelby County Today 137

Conclusion 155
Bibliography 157
About the Author 159

ACKNOWLEDGEMENTS

Any author knows that he or she is only as good as the people behind the scenes offering support and acting as cheerleaders for a given project. I am blessed once again to be surrounded by people who have been committed to helping *A Brief History of Shelby County, Indiana:* to be the best it could be.

To The History Press: Thank you once again for giving me the chance to work with you. I appreciate your openness and your vision for sharing local history in a way that is accessible to a large audience.

To my great-aunts, Virginia Williams and Mary (Toots) Buchanan: I love you both very much and appreciate the memories, photos and knowledge you shared with me for this book. Thank you so much!

To Donna Tracy at the Bluebird Restaurant in Morristown: not only do you make some of the best fried chicken I have ever eaten, but without your photo collection, this book would not have been possible.

To Elaine Gobble: thank you for forwarding me a copy of Mrs. Florence Rock's memories; it truly made all the difference.

To Don Baumgartener, Candace Miller, Rita Rose and the staff at the Genealogy Library in Shelbyville: Your insights made this book come together in a way I couldn't have accomplished on my own. Thanks ever so much!

To John with the Shelby County Alumni Association: thank you for the use of your personal postcard collection!

To Steve Barnett: Thank you for once again working your magic on the text. You are a great friend and I appreciate your insight.

And finally, but most importantly, to my sons, Chris and Vincent: You are always listed last, but rest assured that you are never least. You put up with insane shenanigans from me during this process, and it is amazing that we didn't end up "dazed and confused" by the time it was finished. No matter what I write, you two will always be my finest work, and no woman could be prouder of the men you have become. I love you more…no take backs.

INTRODUCTION

As I put the finishing touches on my third book, *Eastside Indianapolis: A Brief History*, I faced the quandary that plagues all writers the minute one project is complete. *What was I going to tackle next?* For any author who has established a reputation and a following, there is a certain pressure to find new and interesting areas to explore. I liken it to the musician who has all the time in the world to write and record a first hit song and a limited opportunity to conceive a follow-up. Would I take on another history book, or would that long-awaited novel finally emerge from the cobwebbed corner of my hard drive?

The History Press approached me about a book on Shelby County after I waxed on about the beauty of the region. Little did I know what I was getting into when I began my research for this title: Shelby County is an *old* region where family names in the county date back nearly two centuries. It is a history that is intensely protected.

Attempting to take a large county and condense its history into a reasonable volume was a challenge, and I also quickly felt out of my element despite the fact that I had several relatives who lived in Shelby County and friends who grew up in the region. They were all excited about the project and couldn't wait to tell me their personal stories.

This book gave me the opportunity to get some of those stories down on paper that might otherwise have been lost to time. Years ago, I had the chance to interview one of my Shelby County relatives for a college paper, and while I didn't think too much about it at the time, I am grateful now that

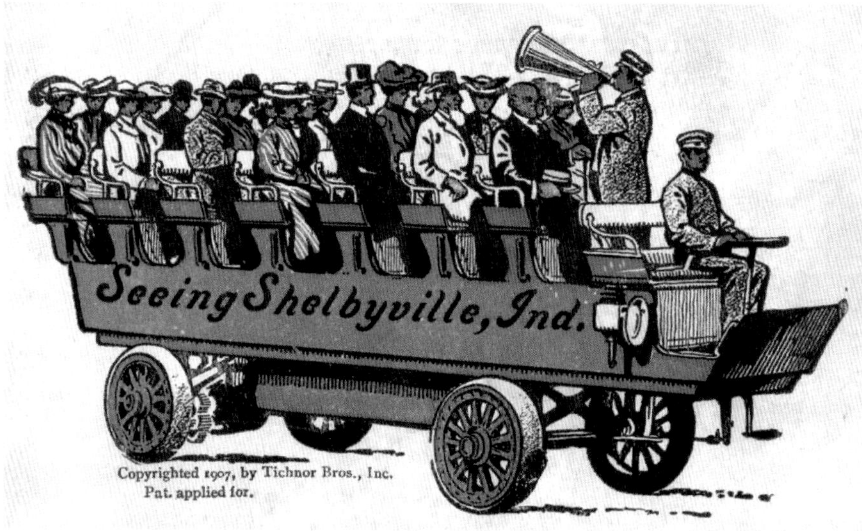

A vintage 1907 Shelbyville postcard advertising tourism in the county.

I saved a copy of the paper as well as the interview tapes so that his story would have a chance to live on in this book. Listening to him speak about growing up in Morel Township and attending school in Morristown during the Great Depression, I gained insight into a time that only exists in grainy news footage or in other history texts.

I couldn't ignore the way his eyes became moist as he described losing a childhood chum to leukemia while in the fourth grade or watching his eyes glaze over when he talked about his experience in World War II (something veterans of that generation *rarely* do). As his voice trailed off and he became lost in his own thoughts, I knew that he was once again that twenty-something-year-old boy fighting for his life on a foreign shore.

His stories also offered me a look into the character that composes the people who live in Shelby County, a class of people who make up the very fabric of what this country is all about. These are the people who worked diligently, who possessed vision and who farmed the land that fed a nation. These core values are something we can still learn from today. Shelby County author Charles Major romanticized the plight of the settlers taming the "wild" land by creating the stories that would captivate the imaginations of Hoosiers for generations. But beyond bears and a Blue River, Shelby County is made up of people who dream big, imagine the possibilities and remain committed to an area that affords them many opportunities.

I wanted to celebrate that through this volume, which showcases the highlights of this community, from the early settlers who were willing to carve a new path and establish pioneer settlements that grew into thriving cities and towns. They were the ones who created their American dream on the outskirts of the Capital City and lived in a place that deserves to be honored not only for its age but also for its contributions to the state of Indiana's central region in terms of industry, agriculture and military history. This tradition continues today, as many troops still deploy through nearby Camp Atterbury, saying goodbye to their families and friends as they answer their country's call.

I will not pretend to have captured everything there is to tell about Shelby County in this small volume, but it is always my hope that my work will help bring history to life in a way that sparks interest from the younger generation and will offer favorite memories to be shared with a larger audience who fondly remember the bygone days. Perhaps we will all learn something new through this book and proudly proclaim, "I didn't know that!"

Chapter 1

Opening the Wilderness

In the decades following the American Revolution, there was a push to move westward beyond the East Coast towns and into the untamed Midwestern region of the country. As new states were being formed, the Kentucky area of the Ohio River proved to be a popular choice for people looking to move into the wilderness while remaining close to a major waterway, which provided the best transportation option for hearty pioneers.

Eventually, settlers migrated north to Indiana, finding its banks along the Ohio an equally ideal place to create homesteads. Even Abraham Lincoln's parents found the area attractive, and its reputation eventually led Indiana to statehood in 1816.

The land that ultimately became Shelby County was Indian territory, so early travelers understood the risks associated with moving through the area if permission was not sought first through tribal elders. White men were not always accepted, and there was the general belief that the "red" man exhibited a thirst for blood. One of the first white men brave enough to conquer the territory was none other than William Conner, a fur trader who moved through the area that is now Shelby County to land farther north, where he settled near present-day Noblesville. (Conner's house is on display at Conner Prairie Living History Museum.)

Conner's brother John was also a trader who conducted a lot of business in Franklin County, where he most assuredly would have been acquainted with some of the earliest names that are now affiliated with

Shelby County, such as Jacob Wetzel and James Wilson. Wetzel has the distinction of being one of the first white travelers through what we know as Shelby County, blazing a trail on foot that would set the area on a course toward its future.

Jacob Wetzel

Wetzel was born on September 16, 1765, as the fifth child of a frontier desperado living in what is now West Virginia. After marrying and starting a family, Wetzel became the sheriff of Ohio County, but personal setbacks forced him to start all over, thus inspiring his westward move.

In 1817, Wetzel purchased land in the western part of Indiana, near the Eel River, that had recently been opened by the government. Rather than use the known waterways to reach his new property, Wetzel negotiated with the Delaware tribe and obtained permission to cross the region on foot. In July 1818, with his son Cyrus Wetzel and companions Thomas and Richard Rush and Walter Banks, Wetzel set off to forge a trail to his new land.

According to published histories, Wetzel's trail moved west from Laurel, crossing Flat Rock River (just seven miles from the area that would become Rushville) and moving beyond the Blue River on the northeast (where

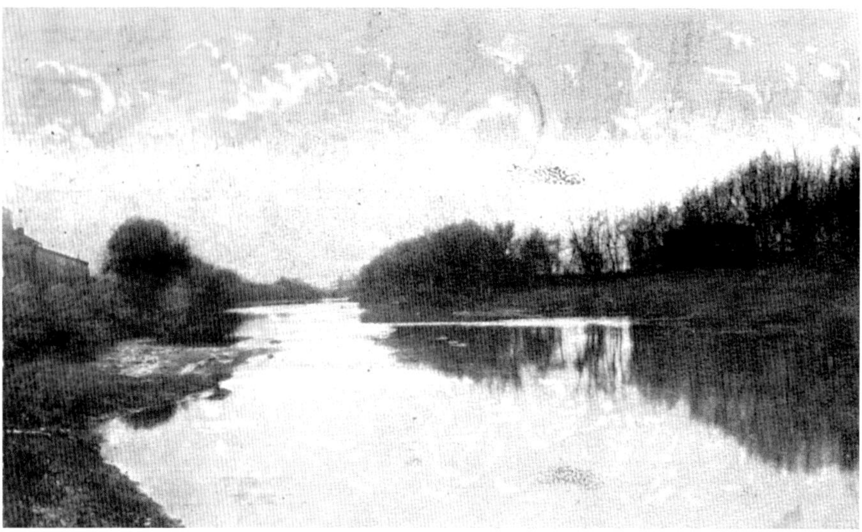

This vintage postcard depicts the Big Blue River below the boat landing.

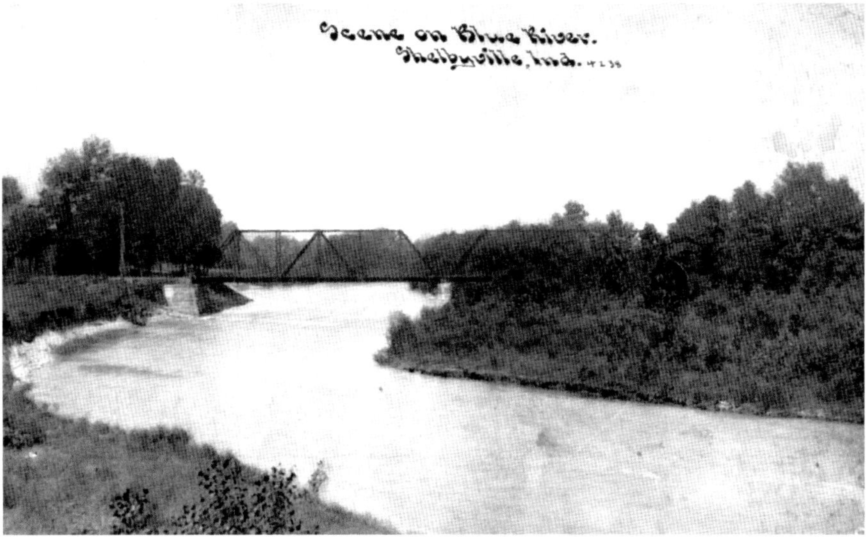

Another scene on the Big Blue River with the bridge crossing over the water.

Shelbyville would eventually be located) on to Sugar Creek, and across Johnson County until they reached the White River.

It was hardly an ideal travel scenario, but the little band made it, and when they finally reached the White River, Wetzel continued on his journey alone while the others returned home to their cabins. Pleased with the results of his foray, Wetzel insisted that the trace be widened in order to accommodate the traffic that one day would use the trail. Others took axes and other crude tools of the day to cut through the dense brush and forests and create what became known as Wetzel's Trace. That original passage was used until 1826, when other roads made the trace obsolete. The presence of fallen trees and other debris created some navigational problems as well. Wetzel's Trace was eventually absorbed into the acres purchased by new settlers to the area, but the forging of the trace remains an important contribution that paved the way for all who were to come to Shelby County.

Early Residents

The trace was an important first step in the development of Shelby County, but so too was the Treaty of St. Mary's. Signed on October 6, 1818, it opened the last of the Indian land in Indiana (including the land that would

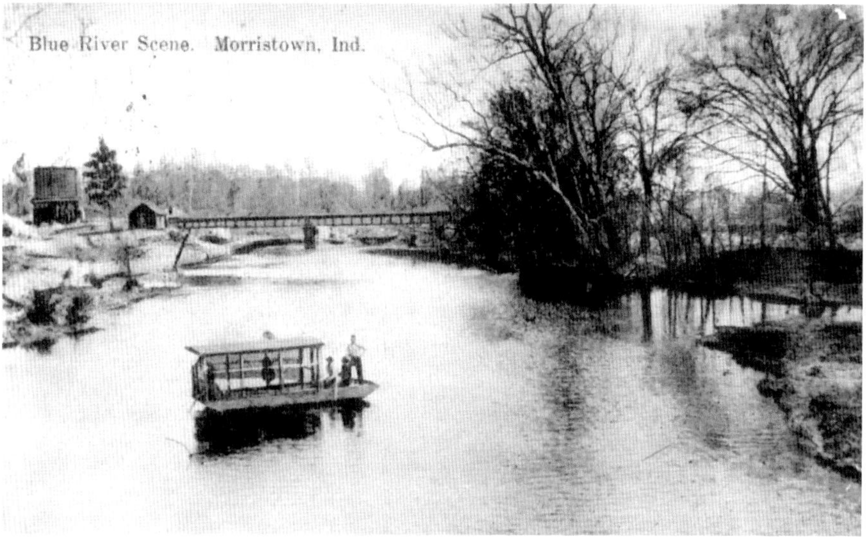

A shot of the Big Blue River as it crosses through the community of Morristown.

become Shelby County) for settlement. The government and the Indians came to an agreement that would enable the Miami tribe to remain in the area for up to three years, and the government agreed to pay the Indians for any improvements made to the land while they inhabited it.

According to Marian McFadden's *Biography of a Town*, few Indians chose to remain for long in the land that would become the Shelby County region, and many were already moving westward by the time the first settlers arrived. There were some stragglers, however, who attempted to establish a life for themselves among the pioneers.

James Wilson was one of those early settlers. Born in 1779, Wilson was the son of a Revolutionary Patriot who moved to Indiana in 1800, first settling in Jefferson County and later moving on to Franklin County. Wilson and his neighbors originally platted the community of Fairfield, but when that settlement didn't develop rapidly, he felt compelled to move on, despite his enthusiasm for his original community.

Wilson heard about Wetzel's Trace and followed the clearing to the Blue River, where he found the perfect spot for his new cabin. That structure would prove to be the first cabin in the county, and it was to this home that Wilson moved his family in 1819. Once they were settled, Wilson set about creating a homestead that his son Isaac remembered in McFadden's work: "James Wilson established a trading post and exchanged coarse clothing, blankets, flints, knives, etc…for the furs the Indians brought in."

In addition to running a busy trading post, Wilson also cleared six acres of land in order to plant a large corn crop that would become very important to the region and remains a vital agricultural component of the state. For a while, Wilson's property was isolated, but by 1820, the area experienced something of a boom when thirteen families joined the Wilsons in determining that this new land was the perfect place to lay down roots. The Berry Trace, cut in 1819, offered an alternative to Wetzel's original trail. While it remains unclear how many settlers might have used the new trace, the additional clearing didn't hurt with the influx of people.

A Capital Change

As the population in Indiana migrated north, there was less of a reason to converge along the Ohio River. This change prompted the legislature to consider reestablishing the state capital in a more centrally located area as opposed to Corydon. In 1820, the decision makers became fond of the area where Fall Creek met the White River and offered plenty of accessibility to the old Indian trails. Though the new capital was nothing more than a dense forest with a few scattered cabins, the legislature was enamored with the new area and settled on the site. It was christened "Indianapolis," a Greek-inspired moniker that wasn't widely embraced by the public, who felt it was simply too fancy.

Not only were people against the name, but there was also a general outcry against moving the capital at all. Thankfully, at least one member of the community, James Gregory, who was elected to the state senate, understood that moving the capital would be good for the growing communities in the area that was soon to be Shelby County. He understood that the commute to Indianapolis would be a lot closer for the residents southeast of the new capital and that being in such proximity would only encourage continued growth for a new county.

Once the capital was relocated to Indianapolis, and with the final acquisition of Indian lands and more settlers moving into the area adjacent to the new city, it was obvious that a local government needed to be formed in order to meet the needs of the residents in the region. In December 1821, the state legislature approved a petition by residents requesting that they be allowed to establish their own county.

This petition, known as "An act for the formation of a new county north of Bartholomew County," contained seven sections that defined the county's boundaries, gave it the name "Shelby County" (after Isaac Shelby, a Revolutionary army officer and the first governor of Kentucky), designated the men who would choose the site for the local seat of justice and selected the Fisher cabin as the initial court building (until a proper structure could be constructed). The measures also provided for the construction of a library and other public buildings, as well as a provision for the election of trustees for the yet-to-be-built edifice.

A New County Seat

Once the county was established, there was a need to create a county seat to serve the populous. Several sites were suggested and considered, including Marion, which James Wilson thought was the obvious choice. But when James Davison, John Hendricks and John Walker offered seventy acres in the middle of the county, the opportunity was too attractive to pass up.

Of the three, Davison was the one with the unremarkable life. Born in Tennessee in 1801, his family moved to Indiana, settling first in Franklin County. When he was an adult, Davison purchased 160 acres just north of the site of Shelbyville and south of the Blue River. After donating a portion of the land for the new town, he bought a farm south of town and lived there until 1855 before moving to Iowa, according to published histories. He ultimately returned to Indiana and bought a farm in Brandywine Township, living there until his tragic death twenty-two years later at the hands of attackers. He died on September 11, 1877.

Major John Hendricks was born into a prominent Pennsylvanian family. His father held many public offices and served several terms in the legislature. After marrying Jane Thompson, Major Hendricks moved his bride near Zanesville, Ohio, then on to Madison and finally to Shelby County, an area in which he had done some surveying work in 1819. He liked what saw, evidently, because in March 1821, he, along with his brother William, entered land at the Brookville office. A year later, Hendricks built a log cabin on the land for his family, living there for ten years before replacing the home with a more sturdy brick structure not far from the original homestead.

In addition to his contribution of fifty acres for the new county seat, Hendricks acquired a great deal of land in the community and ultimately platted an early addition to Shelbyville. As a civic activist, he organized schools, gave generously to church organizations and served as a member of the examination committee for West Point Military Academy. Though he wasn't overly political, he held many offices in the county, including coroner, and was active in the local temperance society. He was even elected to the legislature in 1840.

"He was one of the finest looking men in the state—six feet high, as straight as a rifle barrel, well built up, head large and erect, high forehead, dark hair and thrown back in front, good features, eyes light blue, sparkling and intelligent, he was a noble specimen of the Anglo Saxon race," said Oliver H. Smith, a Connersville lawyer who knew Hendricks in 1822–23.

Hendricks remained committed to the town that he helped to establish until his death on July 24, 1866. His remains were later removed to Crown Hill Cemetery, Indianapolis, where he was reinterred.

John Walker hailed from an Irish family who immigrated to America and settled in Pennsylvania, where he was born in 1787. His father, Benjamin, had a nefarious reputation, and after running into some local trouble with the law concerning the death of an Indian, he relocated to Laughery Creek near Aurora in Dearborn County, Indiana. Benjamin remained productive until he had enough money put aside to send for his family. He operated a mill and built a home for John and the others when they arrived not long afterward. John grew up and married Frances Allen, building a home near his father's place, but the couple moved in 1823. Three years before that move, Walker purchased the land he would eventually donate to the county for the new city.

What is interesting about Walker's story are his contributions to Shelbyville before he ever moved there. He acquired a lot of land in the area and even saw fit to establish the first flour and sawmill to serve the area before it was his home. "The mill stood on the bank of the Blue River, just west of Harrison Street and was the ancestor to several mills which under different ownerships stood on the site well into the 20th century," wrote Charles M. Andrews in his work *The Ancestors and Descendents of John Walker of La Porte, Indiana 1749–1914*.

His acquisitions were not only limited to Shelby County. Walker also purchased 5,120 acres in northwest Indiana in LaPorte County, according to government land office records. He eventually moved there in 1832 and died on August 1, 1844.

As for James Wilson, he was disappointed in the choice of Shelbyville for the county seat. After his hopes of Fairfield fell through, he saw Marion as the obvious choice for the county seat and platted the area. Sadly, it remained "Little Marion" with its lovely public square, and Shelbyville became the area's focal point. Wilson never planned another community before his death in 1824.

The announcement of the choice for the new county seat was made to the public during the Independence Day barbecue of 1822. About two hundred people attended the celebration, which was held just northeast of the modern-day Shelby County fairgrounds. According to Isaac Wilson, while the locals enjoyed a meal of bear, deer and turkey, in addition to entertainment, he couldn't recall much of the day's program, especially the part where the county seat was announced. More than likely, as a young man, he was off swimming and playing with his friends. He did recall that the day "ended in a burst of merriment as a group of settlers formed a circle and passed a fiddle around on which each in turn contributed a tune" before everyone said their goodbyes and headed back to their cabins for the evening, knowing that a new city was about to begin.

Chapter 2

SHELBYVILLE: PRIDE IN PROGRESS

Today, Shelbyville is a city that has it all: great neighborhoods, wonderful city amenities, educational opportunities, technological campuses such as Knauf Insulation and Intelliplex and even a racetrack and casino. It's no wonder the city today deems itself "Pride in Progress" since it hardly seemed likely the city would get off the ground in the early days.

The period following the announcement of the town's selection as the county seat should have been an exciting time for the community, but other than a name, boundaries and an accumulating debt, there was little the town had going for it. At least one early settler realized that without money, decent roads and markets, life in Shelbyville would be hard for its citizens. Dr. Milton Robins was also worried that there could be a fever or cholera outbreak that would take its toll on the populace without adequate resources to properly battle a contagion. "I have often wondered how a community could live with as little money as we had," he said in McFadden's book. "We had nothing to sell, no one had anything with which to buy. Everything was bartered, one dollar would go farther than five or six now, but then it was merely nominal as we rarely handled a dollar."

Plans for the city were nothing but theoretical dreams on paper for a community nestled in swampland, forest and brush. When Able Cole was appointed the first county agent, it was his job to design the first lots and encourage settlers to buy into the new county seat. Henry Gatewood was the first person to buy into the new town, purchasing his lot for fifty dollars. His property was located on the northeast quadrant of the Public Square, where he operated a two-story tavern. No sooner had he set up shop than he was after the county commissioners to construct a road leading from the tavern to his nearby home and farther east to Rushville.

Initially, the limits of the town were small, but as interest in the community grew over the next thirty years, various additions were added. However, the early growth was plagued by financial troubles as well, and the proceeds from Cole's land sales were challenged by the county treasurer. Cole resigned, and the county commissioners appointed Ovid Butler (for whom Butler University is named) to the post.

Butler was well educated, and the commissioners had absolute confidence in his ability to get the community on track. Butler was able to identify some of the problems with the accounting and discovered that there were sixteen unsold lots, which the commissioners advised him to sell (along with other donated outlands) at a public auction in 1830. For the next five years, Butler remained the county agent and performed his job admirably. By 1836, Shelbyville could be described as a thriving community. McFadden notes that one Shelby County resident was quoted as saying there were "between six and seven hundred inhabitants…the buildings were mostly one-story frames, a few log cabins were still standing and brick houses did not number to exceed a dozen." Of course, McFadden also noted that the figures quoted could not always be confirmed and memories often change with time.

Commerce also arrived in the community during this time in order to meet the needs of the growing population. There was at least a dry

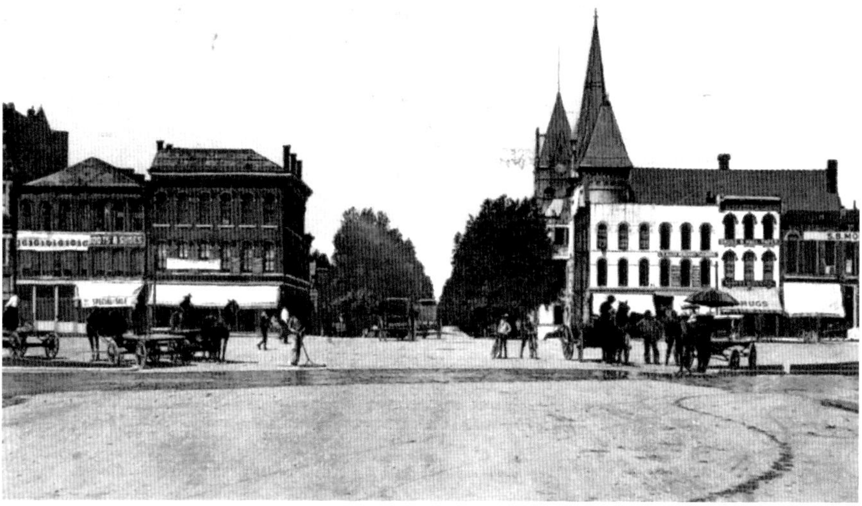

An early shot of the Public Square looking west in Shelbyville, Indiana.

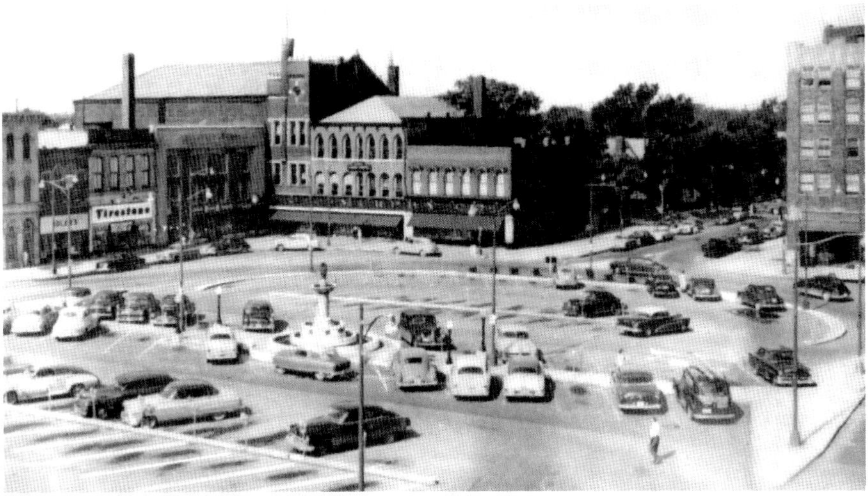

A 1950s postcard depicting a more modern look at the Public Square as it stands today.

goods emporium, a grocery store, a drugstore and a couple of saloons and taverns. (The latter two are considered to be two different types of establishments.)

Throughout the period from 1830 to 1850, those who settled in the area laid down roots that lasted for generations. McFadden wrote that Shelbyville experienced a 123 percent increase in the population during this time, moving from a mere 446 residents to 995, a significant increase for such a young community.

"People who live in Shelbyville tend to stay here," said Don Baumgartner, a Shelbyville resident since 1976. "When my son was little he had a friend who called everyone in town 'aunt' or 'uncle' and my son couldn't believe that anyone could be related to that many people but he had a very large family that remained solidly in the community. That kid was related to practically everyone in town!"

Public Amenities

All of the early governmental meetings concerning the county were held in the homes of its residents, and one of the initial actions taken was to create a stray pound in order to round up wayward animals. A jail was also constructed in those early years, but the major undertaking of the time

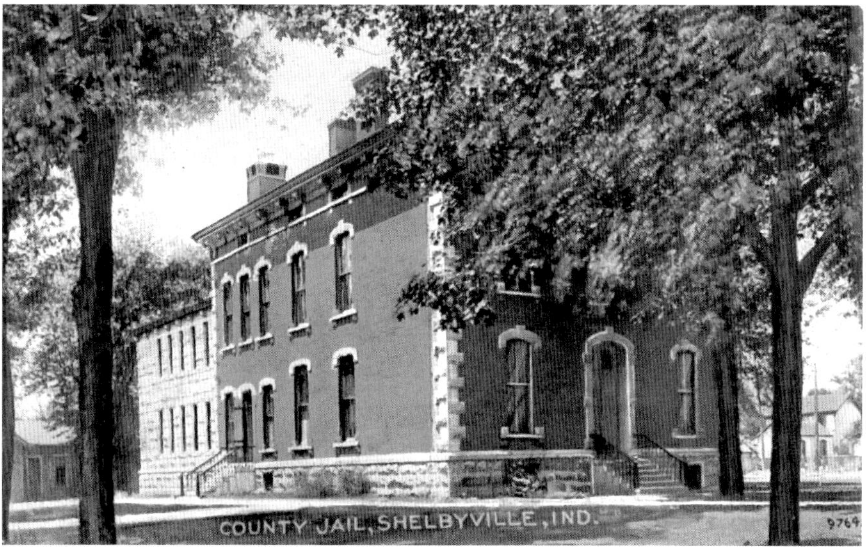

A postcard showing the jailhouse in Shelbyville. The construction of a jail was one of the town official's earliest projects.

was to erect a courthouse in the city that would serve as the home to all governmental affairs. No doubt the grand edifice would have taken a long time to build regardless of the circumstances, but as McFadden recalled, this particular project was nothing short of a "saga."

It took two years for the building to be designed. The plan called for a structure to be forty feet square with a proportional roof, but it was also slated to have other amenities, including a bell, a weather vane and a spire to make the courthouse a standout among the buildings in the town. A plan that was conceived in 1823 finally got underway in 1825, and by November 5, 1827, though the building was far from completed, the county commissioners were finally able to meet within its walls. Butler also oversaw some of the completion of the building, and finally the commissioners accepted the building as "finished" on September 1, 1830. McFadden wrote:

> *The Court was occupying the new building by 1831, though work was by no means completed. It was not until 1833 that the finishing of the interior woodwork was accepted…Why did it take so long? The constructing of the hull alone stretched from 1825–1830 and interior construction dragged on for several more years…With meager equipment and hard-to-get materials, building on the swampy and little cleared terrain surely must have been difficult. Secondly work could be done only when money was available and*

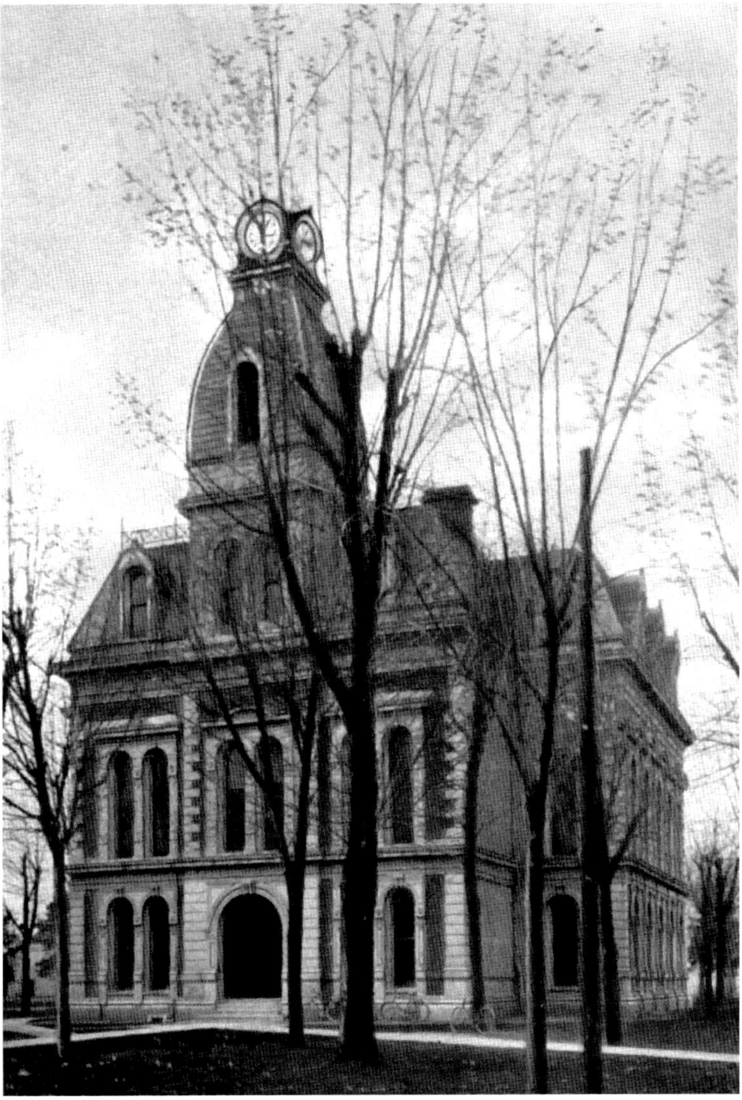

A vintage postcard of the Shelbyville Courthouse. The original building took two years to design and contained many standout features.

> *that was as scarce as the materials and there was no other government that could be called on for financial aid.*

Shelbyville took seriously the need to design infrastructure that would be an asset to the community. Schools are a prime example of that. As expected, the first schools in Shelby County were rural and typical one-room schoolhouses dotting the landscape. The original structures were founded not long after Wilson followed Wetzel's Trace to Little Marion in 1818, though there was no officially organized state school law until 1852. That law would establish a township school system with thirteen divisions. Within those divisions came frame schoolhouses or log construction buildings. Brick buildings did not become prominent until after the Civil War. More impressively, many of these small schools remained operational until the 1930s.

The first school, erected of logs in 1821, was as rudimentary as it gets. Jonathon M. Wilson, son of James, was installed as the first schoolteacher. With twenty-five to thirty students of varying ages, the term was three months long and tuition was seventy-five cents per student. Subjects offered included reading from Biblical text, ciphering via Pike's Arithmetic and spelling using Webster's Speller. The school building itself had a dirt floor and a long fireplace, along with crude benches that couldn't have been very comfortable for learners. There was nothing to lean back on, and the height of the benches had to be difficult for the youngest learners, whose legs dangled to the floor.

Wilson only had six months of learning himself, yet his position as schoolmaster netted him $7.50 each month. There were no separate grades, and everyone learned together, copying their letters using pokeberry juice for ink. Unruly students were kept in line by the harshest methods. Girls were "scolded" and boys suffered under the rod. Parents believed in education, understanding that if a child could read, write and understand numerical equations, he or she was set to succeed in life.

Parents of school-age children in Shelbyville wanted the best education for their children, and the early crude cabin schools simply weren't up to scratch in many mindsets. Trustees and a school board were established in the county in order to help the public school system get off the ground. In 1829, the first district schools arrived in Shelby County. These types of schools continued to be constructed in various districts, but there were some problems as the students couldn't transfer from one school to another due to unclear boundary lines. Because of the poor roads leading to the schools and resulting attendance issues, writings suggest that the students didn't learn much. In the end, the district schools proved to be a failure. In 1848, every citizen voted for a better school system, and as the laws changed, more provisions were added to ensure that every boy and girl would receive a better education.

George Billman wrote in *The School History of Marion Township*, "For a period of time before and after the Civil War, there was a short period known as the frame school house period." Thanks to the amount of timber, mills and skilled carpenters around, it was possible to construct a number of schools. Of course, by 1870, most of the timber was gone. "A few years prior to this date," wrote Billman, "Mathias Schoelch, an enterprising German, started a brick yard on the south side of Shelbyville." His ingenuity ushered in the brick schoolhouse era.

The new school system meant that the three-trustee system was abolished and only one trustee was elected. Leander Kennedy was among the first trustees in 1880. The first school superintendents, who couldn't read or write, were really school examiners. Eventually, these gentlemen were replaced by educated businessmen who were more suited for the job.

Most of the early schoolhouses held grades one through eight, and eventually a few of them included a couple of years of high school as well. If further education was desired, then students were free to attend the high school in Shelbyville, Rushville or Columbus.

Hilda Morris attended one of these one-room brick schoolhouses and recorded her memories in *The Schools that Grew America*. She wrote, "The average red brick room was 25' by 40' by 15' rectangle with three tall windows

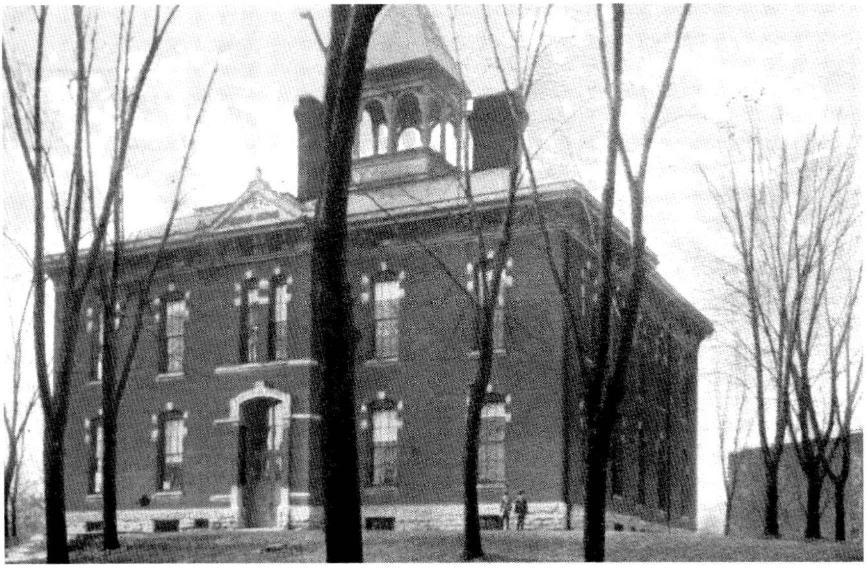

A vintage postcard of Public School number 3 in Shelbyville. Original schools were rudimentary log cabin varieties.

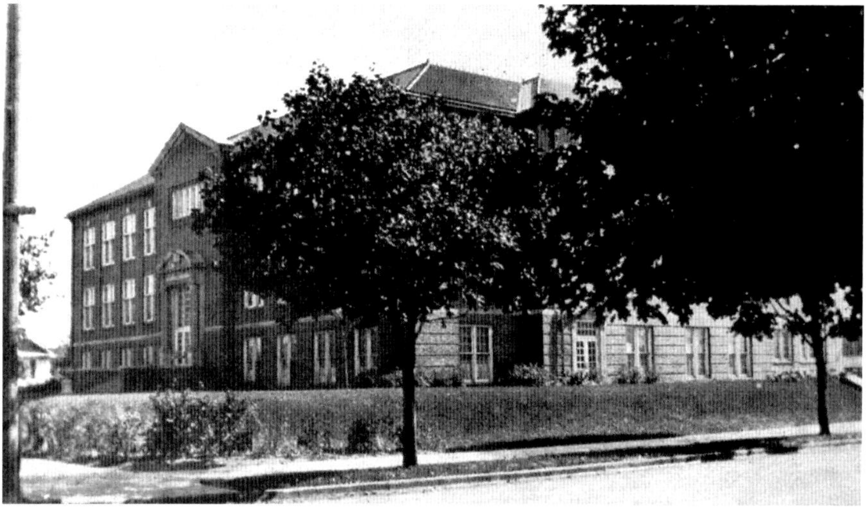

A postcard of Shelbyville High School. The original facility was constructed in 1896.

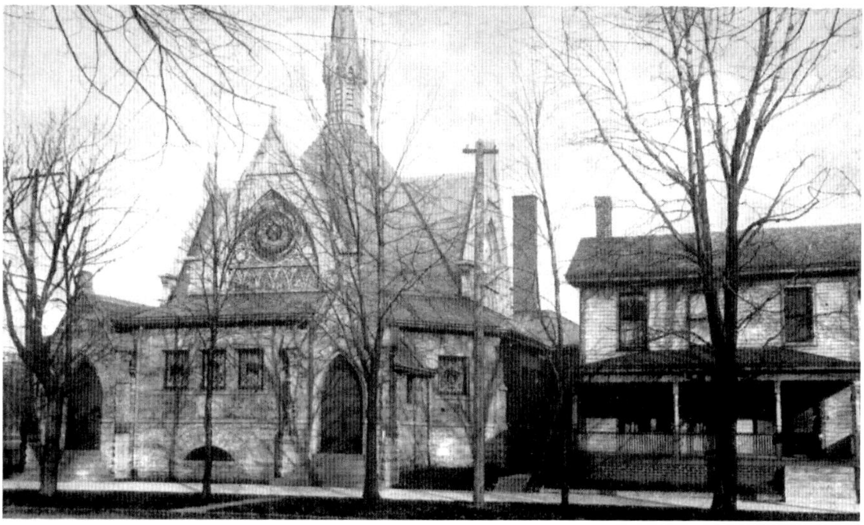

A postcard of the First Christian Church in Shelbyville.

on each side of the two long sides…a rectangular box shaped stove was centered in the back third of the floor…fuel was fairly cheap and plentiful and clothing made up the difference…of course a bare cold cedar floor did not generate much heat either."

There were thirty to forty-five desks in a variety of sizes. Promotion from one grade to the next meant that a change of rows or desks was in order. Slate blackboards accommodated multiple grades of work, including seventh-grade English, fourth-grade math and enough remaining space for the instructor to make notes for a history lesson. Other amenities of these new, modern schoolrooms included an unabridged Webster's Dictionary, a clock, maps, a glove and a school "library" containing books such as *Uncle Tom's Cabin*, *Aesop's Fables* and *Samantha at Saratoga.*

"We began preparing for school by the end of July," Morris wrote. "New, practical, homemade clothing consisted of two dark wool dresses made by mother and tried on during the hot August weather, four to five light percale full cover aprons [and] the latter days of August required a special trip to town to buy books…pencils…thick scratch tablets and at least four penpoints."

Morris said that each morning her mother would pack their lunches in their lunch pails, and then it was up to the children to make sure that the food lasted until lunchtime. In 1890, most of the schoolteachers were men, and entertaining yourself on the playground meant finding "equipment" with whatever happened to be around. Her memories suggest that going to school in Shelby County was a wonderful experience and worth every moment.

As residents settled and homes and businesses began dotting the landscape, it was only natural that church organizations became prominent additions to the community as well. The citizens of Shelbyville relied on their faith congregations to provide spiritual sustenance during those early years.

One of the first denominational churches was founded in 1825 by Elisha Mayhew and six other congregants. The First Methodist Church was known for hosting some of the most prominent pioneer preachers of the day, including John Strange. Initially, the congregation met in homes, as well as the courthouse and a local schoolhouse on Franklin Street, before deciding that a permanent home needed to be constructed to accommodate the congregation. A lot was purchased on the corner of Mechanic and Tomkins Streets. The frame building constructed on the site was used until 1852, when a new building was erected on Washington Street.

According to McFadden, Zebulon Wallace's cabin served as the first meetinghouse for the Presbyterians in Shelbyville. The congregation comprised thirteen members and a traveling minister. Eventually, Elipalet Kent was assigned to the church. He would prove to be a long-term resident of the community and contributed a lot to the spiritual and educational lives of those in the city. Kent and his wife, Fannie, moved to Shelbyville, living first in a two-room cabin that was owned by Sylvan Morris. The couple

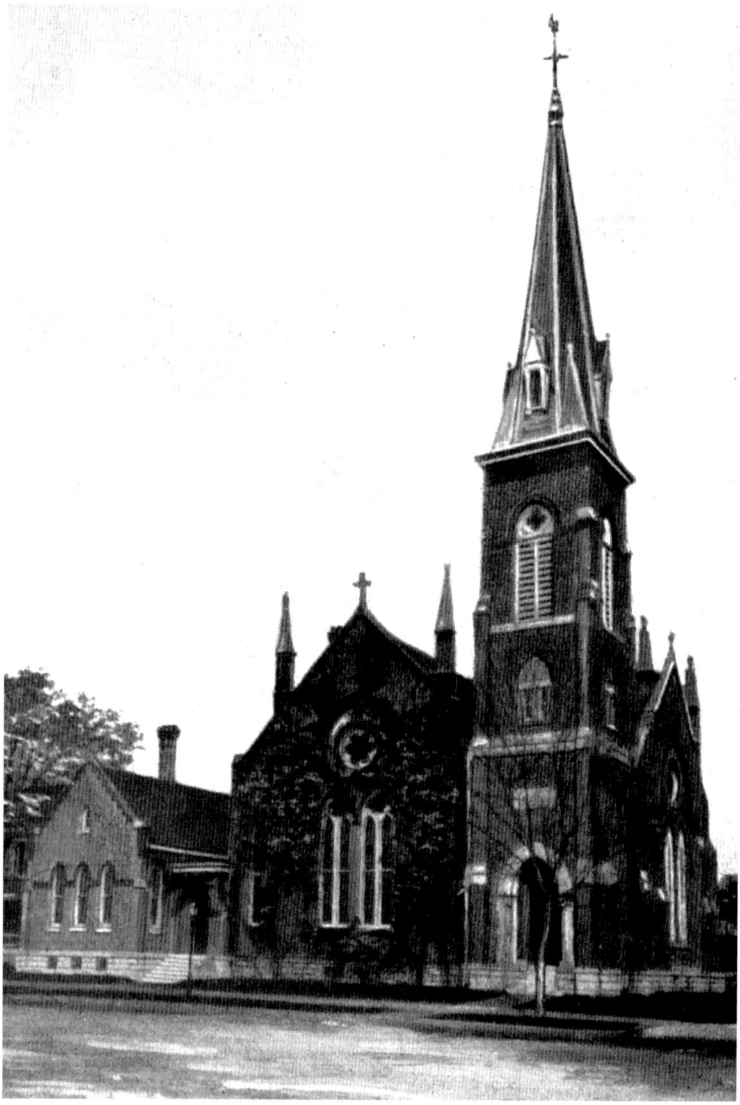

A vintage postcard showing the First Presbyterian Church of Shelbyville.

eventually moved into a two-story brick home that was located across from the post office. McFadden wrote:

> *The building was constructed by John Walker and John Hendricks, with some financial assistance from others, in order to provide a more adequate school for their children and suitable quarters for a teacher. It was probably*

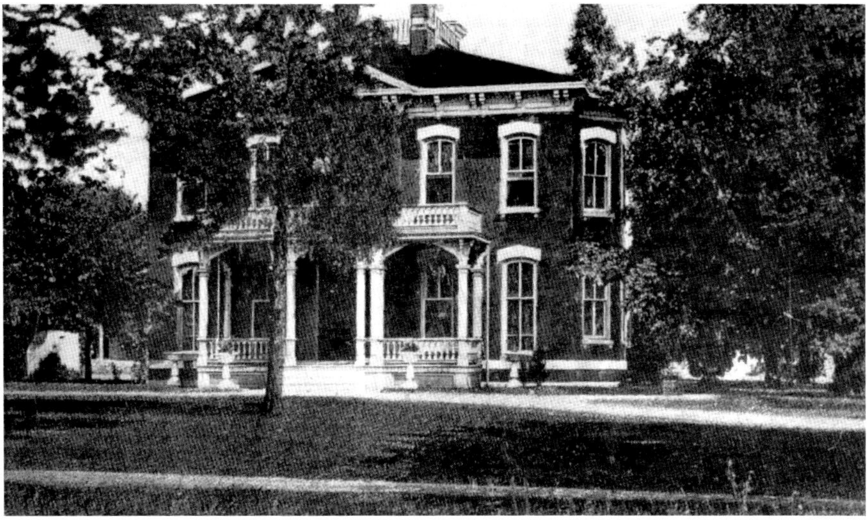

Though labeled the "Elks Home," this postcard shows one of the elegant buildings constructed in Shelbyville during the late 1800s.

> *built after the Kents came and the sponsors recognized in Fannie, the instructor they so badly needed. In 1830 Kent wrote to a fellow minister in Virginia, "I live in my own red house made of brick, one room below and one above. Mrs. Kent is at present teaching school in a lower room, growing quite popular. The upper room is my study."*

The Kents lived in Shelbyville, ministering to several congregations, but in 1835, the couple moved to Greenwood only to return to Shelbyville in 1839, about the same time that it was decided that a permanent Presbyterian church needed to be built. The site chosen for the church was at Jackson and Harrison Streets. The initial building was a frame structure that featured a "roof surmounted by a cupola and in that cupola was a bell purchased with some money raised by some of the women in the congregation," wrote McFadden.

The Methodists and Presbyterians were the dominant congregations in the Shelbyville area, but soon there were Baptists among them as well. Catholics followed. The first Baptist church was established in 1849, while the Christian congregation met in Ovid Butler's house. The Catholic St. Vincent Church was an extensive parish that extended to the Indianapolis area.

"Civil" Unrest

The period of complacent growth and stability was rattled when Fort Sumter was fired upon and the nation became embroiled in the Civil War. Shelbyville's initial enlistees joined the Seventh Regiment, rallying to the Union's banner full of high hopes, but, sadly, many of them would not return, and many of those who did were wounded or disease-ridden.

The initial excitement of the war led to the formation of many companies, as well as a company of the Home Guard, but as the casualties mounted and the war drew closer to home in 1863, fewer men were signing up. McFadden wrote, "In July John Morgan and his raiders crossed the Ohio and were ravaging Southern Indiana. By Sunday, July 12, their entrance into Shelbyville was expected momentarily." The *Banner* reported that there were a number of rumors going around and no one knew what to believe.

In the end, Morgan turned back without ever entering the county, and in time the news of recent victories in the South were enough to keep the spirits of the citizens high. Still, the action didn't stop. Soldiers returning home were soon back on the battlefield. During their furloughs, they would bring home stories of soldiers who went off to war and would never see their families again.

In total, 3,120 Shelby County sons enlisted, with 200 losing their lives in the conflict. County commissioners knew that the family members of those serving in the war would need assistance, and funds were set aside to help the needy during this time. McFadden said private aid was also sought: "As always, the women worked to provide comforts for the men away from home…they collected 10 boxes of supplies for the wounded, containing sheets, pillow slips, towels, bandages, soap, fruit and other foods…in 1862 a Soldiers Aid Society of Shelby County was formed…to aid the destitute, sick, wounded, disabled soldiers and their families."

No matter if you had a family member in the war or not, the Civil War was a tumultuous time in the county's history. Prices were high and supplies were short. Taxes were also a problem that effectively deterred some citizens and crippled business. In spite of the difficult economy, new businesses opened while established ones continued in operation.

When General Lee's surrender was announced, celebrations broke out around town, but it was short-lived as not long after, the assassination of President Lincoln cast a pall over the nation. Lincoln's body lay in state in Indianapolis, and a number of Shelbyville residents made the pilgrimage to see the slain president.

The soldiers returned, and life went on. Some of them created veterans' organizations while other groups campaigned to have a monument built to commemorate the soldiers' sacrifices in the war. The black moment in the county's history was over.

Between Wars

The period between the Civil War and World War I offered a welcome peace to Shelbyville. Despite the hardships and shortages caused by the war, growth in the postwar era saw many homes constructed. In fact, during the opulent Victorian/Edwardian period, some of the most beautiful houses were erected.

One notable home was that of George Thatcher, a brick residence just off the square on Washington Street. An entrepreneur and member of the legislature, upon his death in 1885, Thatcher's sister continued to reside in the home until she died in 1917. The home was eventually purchased by the First Methodist Church and used as a parsonage until the building was razed in 1958.

Washington Street was also the location of Alfred Major's home. Designed to be a replica of his wife's home in Pennsylvania, this grand

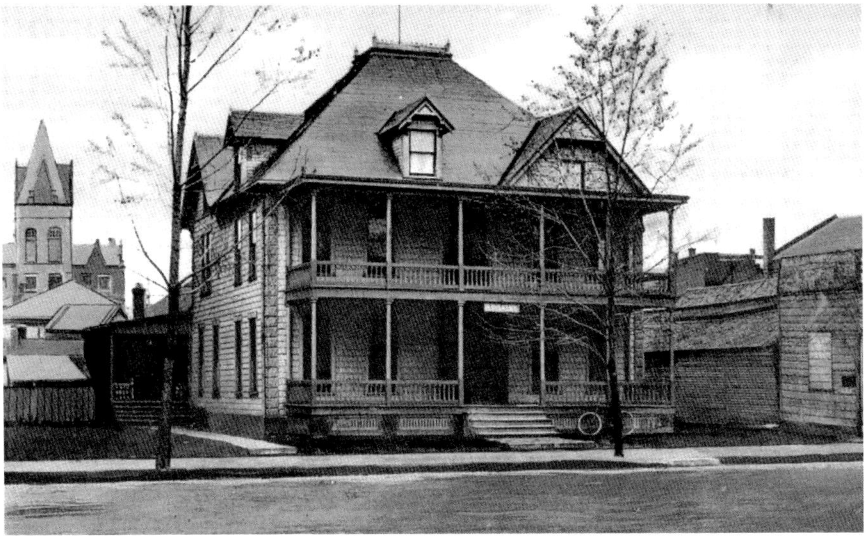

The BFOE Home is another example of the charming houses that were constructed throughout Shelbyville near the end of the Civil War era and beyond.

house possessed a third-floor ballroom and imported interior appointments. Sadly, Major died before the home could be completed, and his wife never lived there. His son took over the residence, and it became home to the younger generation of Majors.

It was an idyllic time to be a part of Shelby County. Families attended church together, and neighbors had time to visit on the front porch. Young lovers walked along lover's lane or took in amusements at the county fair. In those days, children gathered on neatly kept lawns, playing croquet or a quick game of hide-and-seek before returning home for the night; however, the good times were not meant to last, as the Great Flood of 1913 was on the horizon, loudly ending the quiet time that had been enjoyed by so many.

The Great Flood

January 1913 had already been wet, with a record 6.14 inches of rain falling. A soggy March followed, adding to the already soaked terrain and hemorrhaging the rivers. Flooding was all too commonplace in Shelbyville, but nothing quite like this. "After several days of continuous rain, a veritable deluge began around 2 a.m…resembling a water spout," wrote McFadden.

The fire whistle blew a warning to residents as they swung into action, filling sandbags and preparing for the worst. "That morning as the town realized the seriousness of the situation, ordinary business was suspended. All available men, horses, vehicles, and supplies were commandeered to strengthen the levees; boats and rafts were used for rescue work and the waters continued to rise," said McFadden.

As the water poured through the city, residents relying on modern conveniences like electricity were wishing they were like their neighbors who still relied on gas and kerosene for light. Trains couldn't function, and the neighboring cities were dealing with floods of their own and couldn't offer any assistance. The mayor of Chicago at the time actually wired Mayor Hawkins in Shelbyville pledging his assistance, but Hawkins politely told him that the town would remain self-sufficient, a sign of Shelbyville's robust tenacity.

Amazingly, there were no deaths as a result of the great flood; however, there were a few problems, including a birth that had to be dealt with and a housing crisis for the more than two thousand people who suddenly found themselves homeless in the rain.

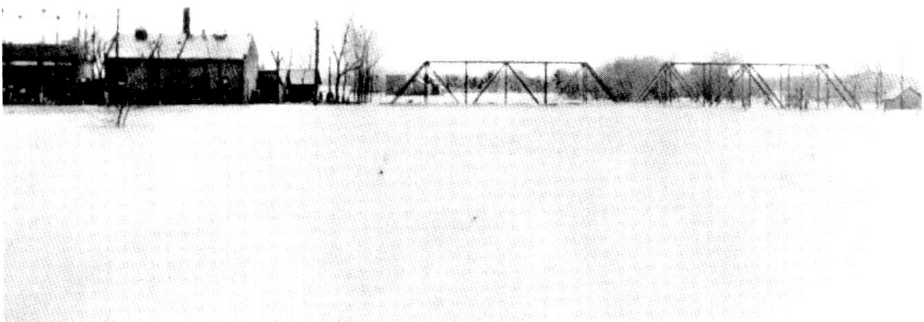

This vintage postcard shows the damage from the Great Flood of 1913.

"By the evening of the 25th, the waters begun to recede, due to the breaking of the levee at Freeport which relieved the pressure downstream...The next morning refugees, not wanting to depend on 'charity' started out for home, but home many of them learned was a mass of mud and debris," McFadden wrote. Many of them had to return to the relief centers.

"My neighbor who was here since 1904 told me that the water got as high as my third step on the back porch," said Don Baumgartner. "To this day, I have to have flood insurance because of it."

After the Rain

The Great Flood signaled the end of the quiet period, and the early portion of the 1900s began to see an increase in the suffragist movement campaigning for the right of women everywhere to be allowed to vote. In addition, a political assassination far away in Europe was about to bring a clash of the great powers that was to become "the war to end all wars"—World War I.

It's no surprise that there was a rush of patriotic spirit and a huge swell of attendance at local church services. Emotions were high over the war, and it wasn't long before recruitment centers, bearing a stern invitation by Uncle Sam, were swamped by the men of Shelby County, who once again answered the call to serve their nation. During one drive, 2,036 men enlisted

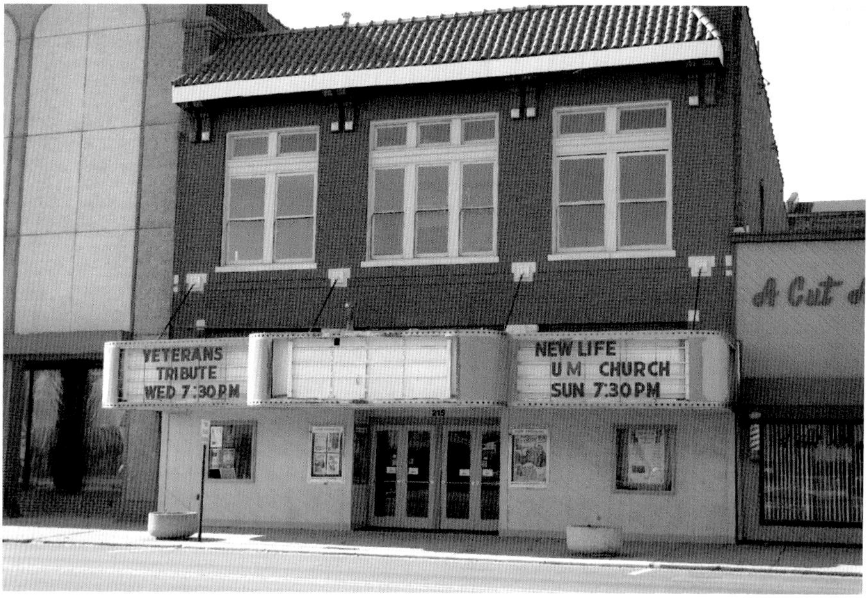

The Strand Theatre offered Shelbyville plenty of cultural offerings in its early years. Today, it has been refurbished and serves as a live music venue. *Author's private collection.*

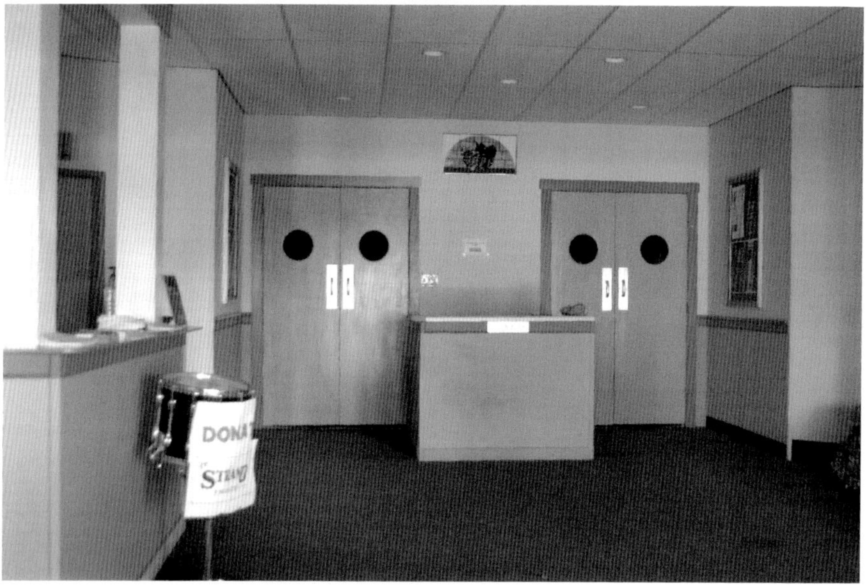

and shipped out from Fort Benjamin Harrison in Indianapolis. Women's groups joined the Red Cross rolling bandages and gathering supplies for the boys fighting "over there."

It was also a time when glorious buildings were constructed, including the Strand Theatre. According to its website, the Strand Theatre

> *has been a mainstay of the Shelbyville, Indiana cityscape since 1916. With the exception of the transition period beginning in the spring of 2005, the Strand has been in continuous operation since opening in the spring of 1916. It is the only surviving "old" theatre in the city limits of Shelbyville. MainStreet Shelbyville, Inc., acquired the building from its owners in the summer of 2004 to help preserve this important part of our local history. There was a strong sentiment among the board members of this group that if this important step were not taken, the building could possibly be lost to history.*

A short article was written about the Strand in the *Shelbyville Republican* in 1915, which read in part, "The Dorsey Brothers, William V. and S.L. Dorsey, and their mother have signed a contract with William Meloy for the erection of a building to be used by Mr. Meloy as a moving picture theatre. Much has been said about this proposed building…The building will take out two stories of the livery stable building but will support the third story of that building. In every respect the theatre building will be modern."

In 2006, a transition team was developed in order to transfer ownership of the Strand and its assets to the Strand Theatre of Shelbyville, Incorporated, in order to renovate, rejuvenate and operate the Strand Theatre. Their petition was approved, and those involved with the Strand, in addition to the community members, got to work on the building, which is now a live performing arts center and can once again be enjoyed by multiple generations for years to come.

Despite the excitement of the theatre during the early part of the 1900s, the real drama continued to unfold in Europe. The war saw rising prices on the homefront and other hardships, not to mention bitter weather that made everything else seem a little bit worse. Sacrifices had to be made by the populace in order to ensure that there would be enough supplies for the troops. Families were asked to go "gasless" on Sundays in order to save fuel, which led to a resurgence of the horse-and-buggy days. Those on the homefront also made do by donating old clothes and growing their own food in order to cope with shortages.

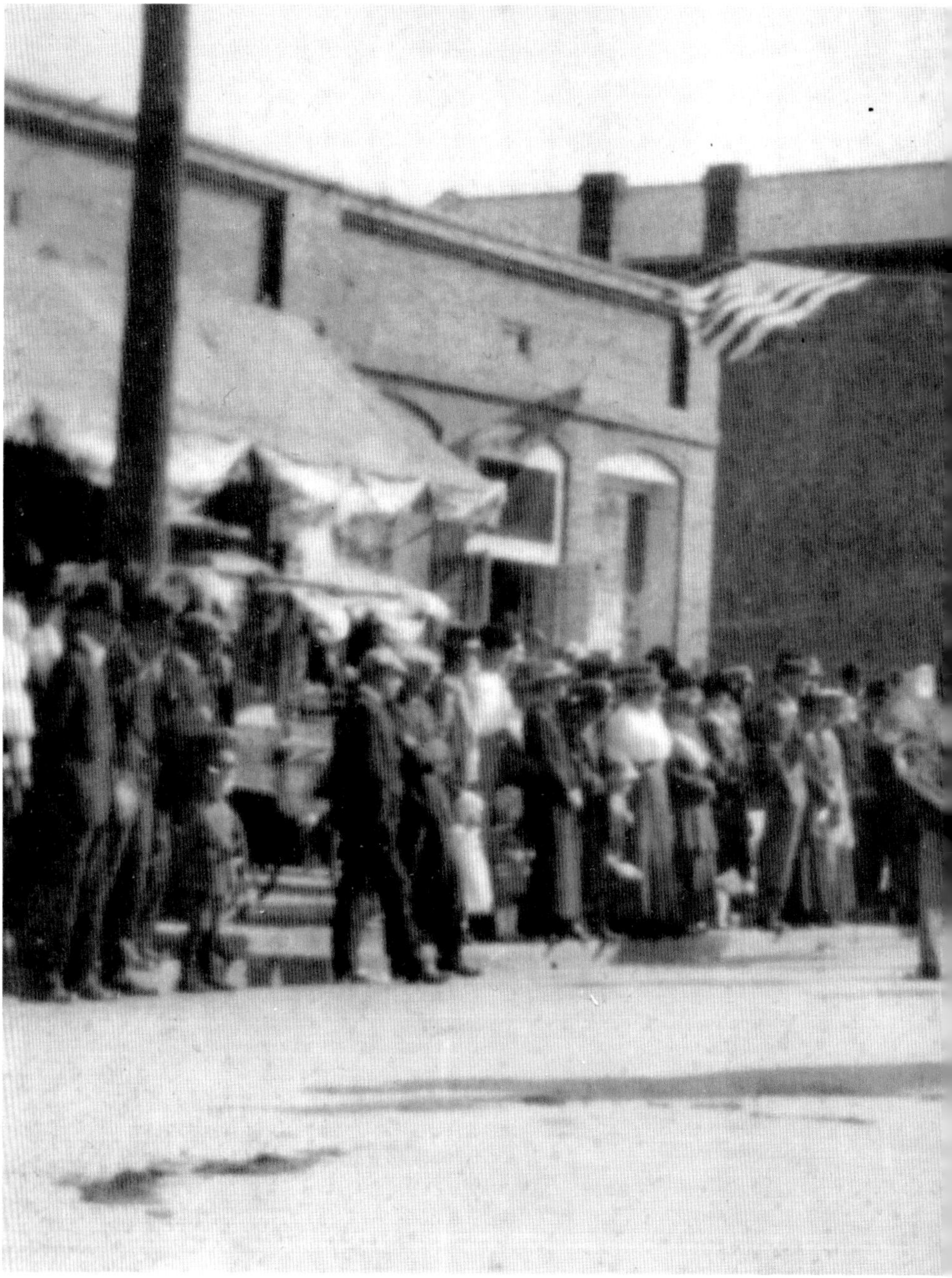

A rare postcard showing Armistice Day, November 11, 1918, in Morristown. *Courtesy of Donna Tracy at the Blue Bird Restaurant.*

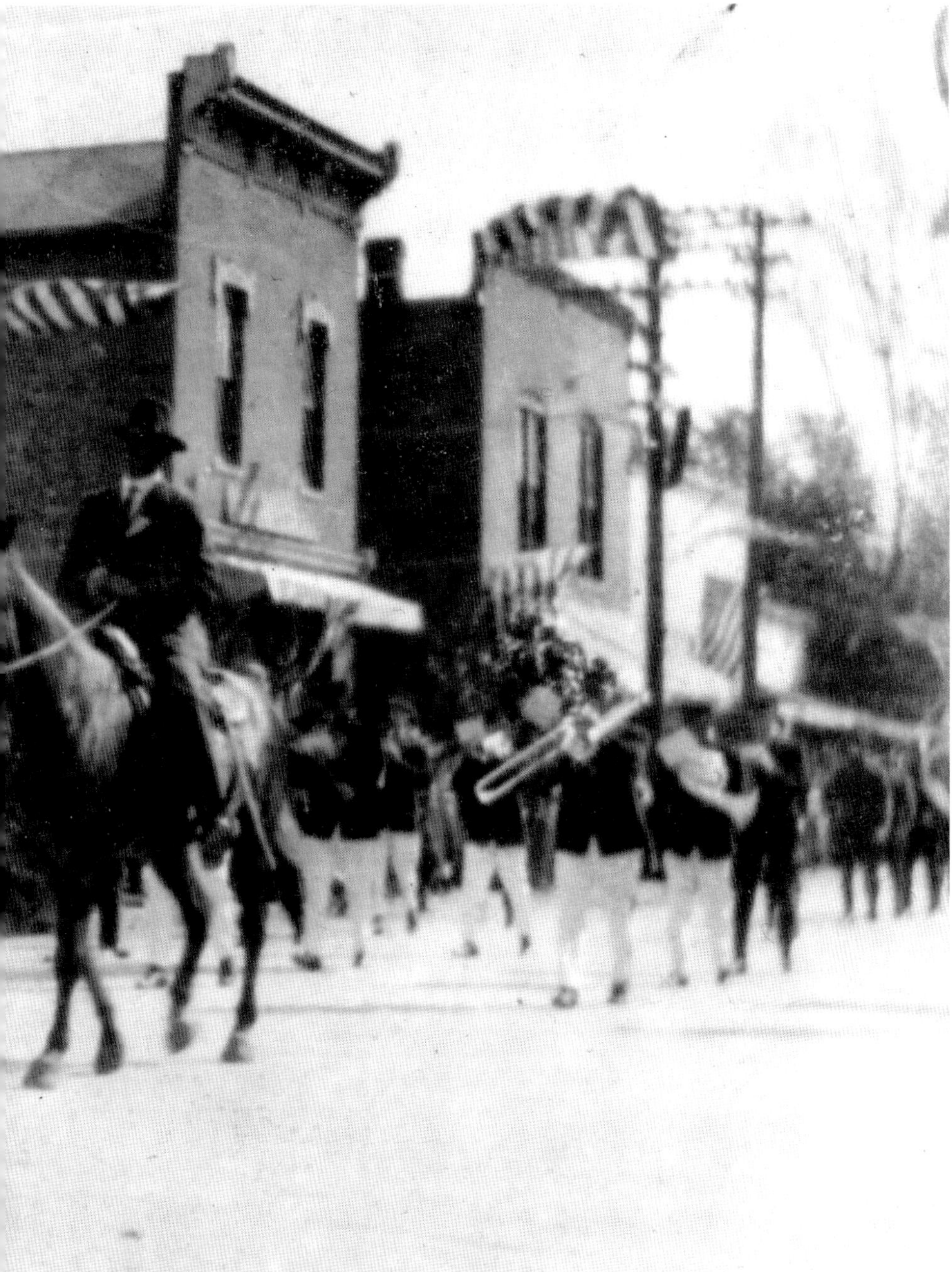

The nation celebrated Armistice Day on November 11, 1918, and Shelbyville was right there ready to welcome the county's soldiers home with open arms. As the vets returned, they established local chapters of national servicemen's organizations, such as the American Legion, which still has a significant presence in the community today.

Time to Live

The Roaring Twenties saw the emergence of more service groups in the Shelbyville community. The Boy Scouts of America began in 1915, and service organizations such as the Masons and Odd Fellows were still going strong and were joined by other adult leagues such as the Rotary Club (1920), Kiwanis International (1925) and the Lions Club (1929). To the average person, it would seem that life was only getting better in the twenties, but there were a few drawbacks to living in this exciting time. The Ku Klux Klan boasted a huge presence in the state and was actively recruiting members. The Klan arrived in Shelbyville with bedsheets and burning crosses, but for an organization so vigorous in other parts of Indiana, it really didn't create much of a splash in Shelbyville.

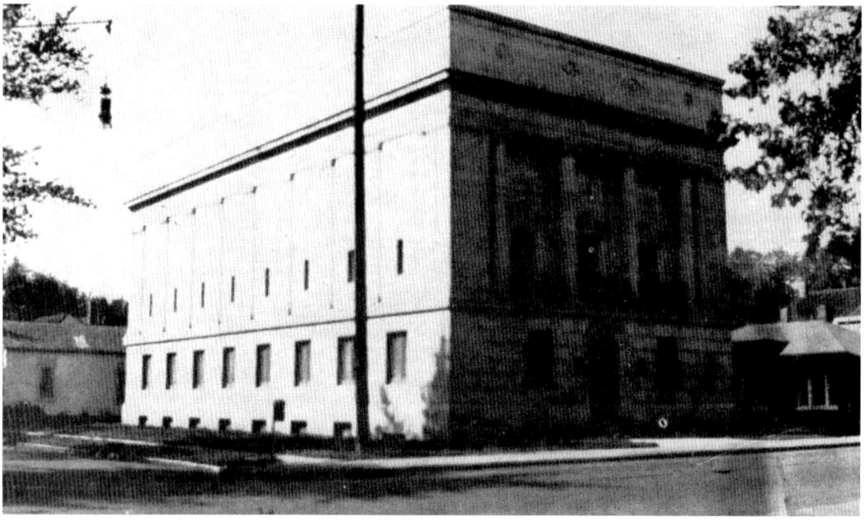

The Masonic Lodge Hall in Shelbyville. Despite humble beginnings over a storefront, the Masons established themselves as one of the earliest service groups in the community.

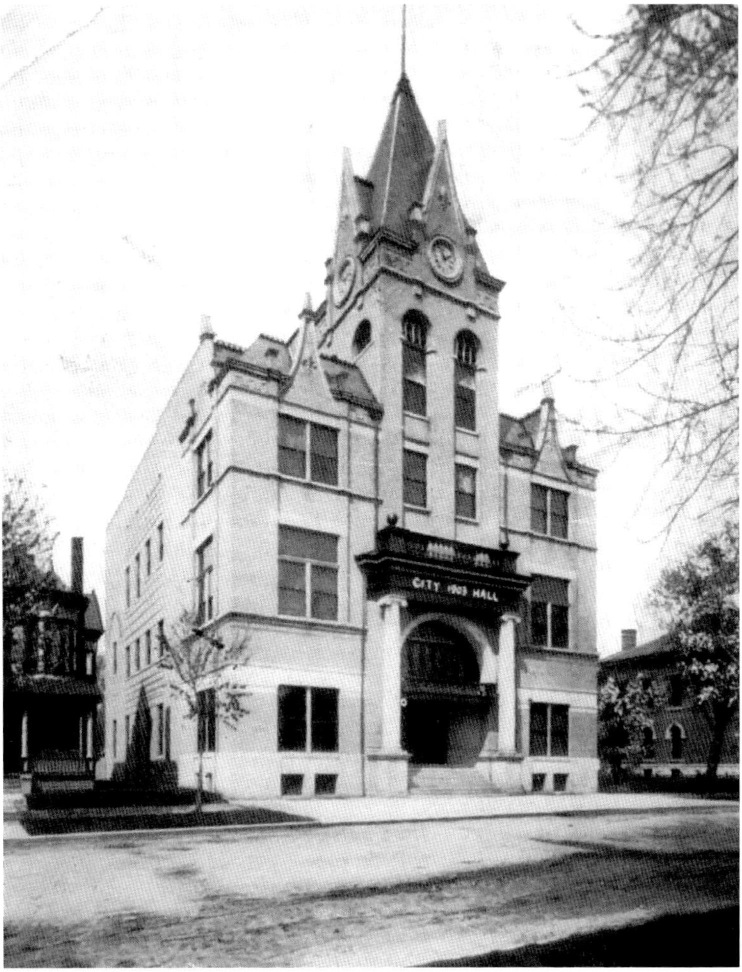

An old city hall postcard showing an early version of the building.

A major fire also destroyed city hall and caused damage to several homes along Tompkins Road. Though the municipal building had to be relocated for a time while the damaged building was being reconfigured, most of Shelbyville was merely grateful that no one was hurt. After all, it had only been a week before that nine hundred children had been at a Christmas party in that building. The alternative could have been an unimaginable disaster for the town.

Healthcare was desperately needed in the Shelbyville community. When William S. Major died in 1915, he specified in his will that his home should be donated to the city for the purpose of building a hospital. While his wife followed up on that bequest, it wasn't until January 1920 that the physicians of Shelbyville organized a hospital association and purchased another property west of the Major home on which to build the new facility. The plan was to use the Major home as an administrative building. Not long after, the Indiana General Assembly passed special legislation that allowed the city to begin work on the project. Once the enthusiasm for the hospital was renewed, Mrs. Major again offered her home for use, and this time, the physicians accepted the donation.

Mrs. Major remained in a room just off the entrance to the hospital until her death, though in 1922, she deeded the property to the city. Once that occurred, an architectural firm was hired to build a hospital addition and to make the necessary changes to the home. According to Major Hospital's website:

> *The hospital was opened officially for public visitation on June 18 and 19, 1924. The first patients were received on June 21, 1924. From 1924 until 1947, the official governing body for the hospital was the Shelbyville Board of Health. From 1924 to 1932, a city tax levy varying from $0.20 per hundred in 1924 to $0.04 in 1932 helped make up any deficits in hospital financing. Interest from a steadily growing endowment also helped keep the hospital solvent. This endowment fund reached $100,000 in 1931 and is several million dollars today.*

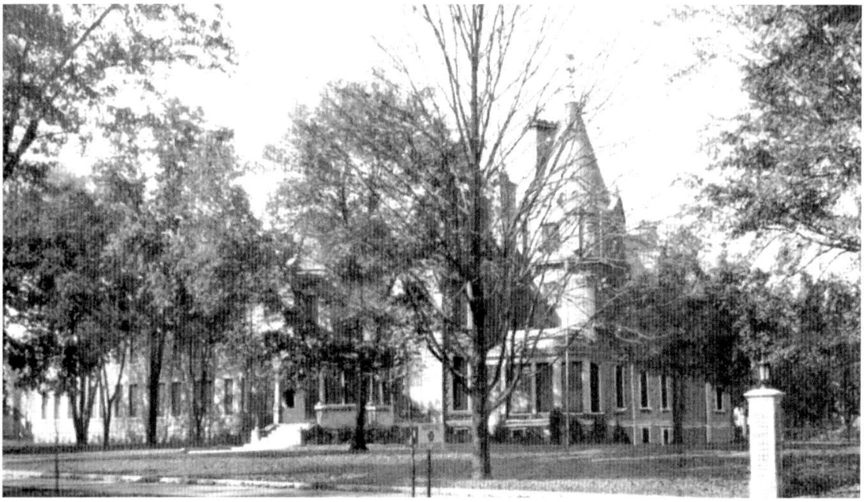

Over the years, Major Hospital has proven to be a vital part of the healthcare system of Shelby County.

During the Great Depression (discussed in greater detail later), the hospital was able to survive by cutting its costs throughout, including the closing of the nursing home, reducing staff and asking employees to take a cut in pay. Superintendents came and went as several women who held the posts were offered other job opportunities or chose to get married. In 1947, the fifty-bed hospital was expanded in order to make way for nursery facilities. When the ward was completed, twelve of the seventeen new cribs were filled with infants.

In April 1956, the hospital faced another expansion. Due to crowded conditions, hospital officials considered moving the hospital to a new location on the outskirts of the city. In the end, it was decided that the hospital would remain and that two new wings and a kitchen facility would be added at a cost of $1,441,000. The expanded hospital opened in the summer of 1960.

Over the years, many exciting things have happened around Major Hospital. The Major Hospital Foundation was established in 1961, and state-of-the-art units were added, including an intensive care unit and physical therapy department. However, there was almost another immediate need for expansion. In 1976, it was decided that a new facility would be built behind the original hospital on Franklin Street. Some of the original portions of the hospital were razed, including Major's home, but the 1960 wings were retained and renovated. Other improvements in the new facility were stained-glass windows, a new chapel and limestone facing pieces, as well as extensive landscaping plans. The new building was ready for use in 1981.

In the later part of the twentieth century, Major has become a leading force in the healthcare of south central Indiana. According to its website, Major showed the results of a two-year project with the opening of the Rampart Professional Center to the public in December 1997. This facility is able to house sixteen doctors, including specialists in family medicine, pediatrics, orthopedics, internal medicine and obstetrics/gynecology. A pharmacy, X-ray office and dental office are also in the center. This $5.5 million renovation is part of Major Hospital's effort to attract more physicians to Shelbyville."

The hospital also boasts a fantastic thirty-nine thousand square feet on its third floor. This is advantageous because it enables Major to house all of its women's services in a convenient location apart from the rest of the hospital offerings.

"Major Hospital has become a forerunner of information technology, named one of the top 100 information system hospitals in the United States. Using the latest technology, doctors have more access to patient information, leading to better patient care," says the hospital's website.

MODERN CITY, SMALL-TOWN CHARM

Throughout the twentieth century, Shelbyville strove to modernize its offerings while still enjoying its reputation as a small town. Over the years, many industries have called Shelbyville home, including production plants like the Coca-Cola Bottling Company, General Electric, Guide Signal & Light, as well as others. During the Great Depression, some of these companies folded or fell onto hard times, while others, like the Indiana Stove Company, secured government contracts and contributed to the national defense during World War II.

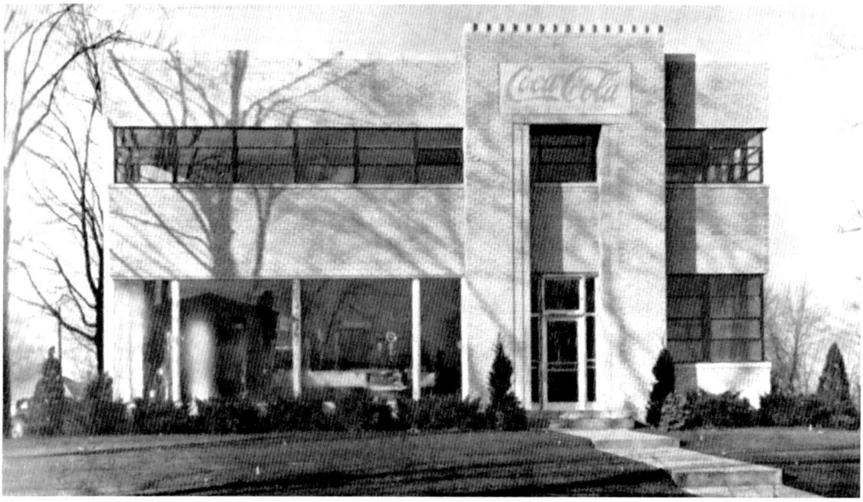

It's the real thing! A postcard of the Coca-Cola Bottling Plant located in Shelbyville.

Opposite, top: The Shelbyville Conrey-Davis Factory, taken by C.O. Williams of Bloomington, Illinois.

Opposite, middle: The Kennedy Car Liner & Bag Company in Shelbyville, one of the largest producers of handmade bags in the world.

Opposite, bottom: Spiegel Factories in Shelbyville, taken by C.O. Williams of Bloomington, Illinois.

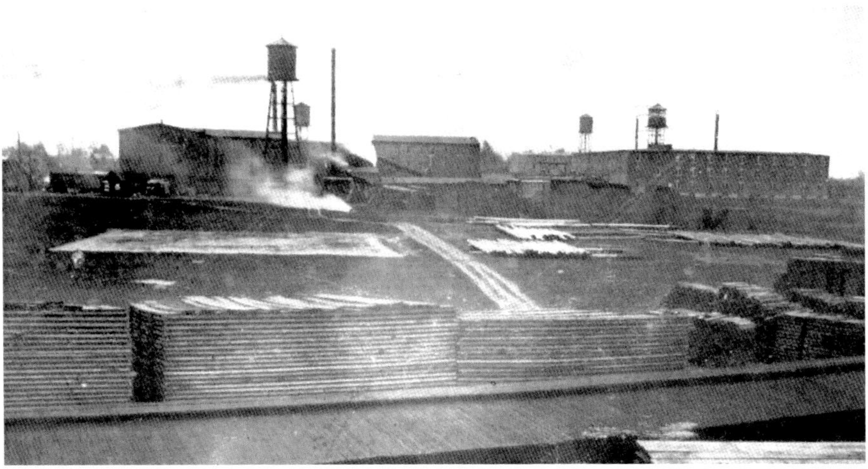

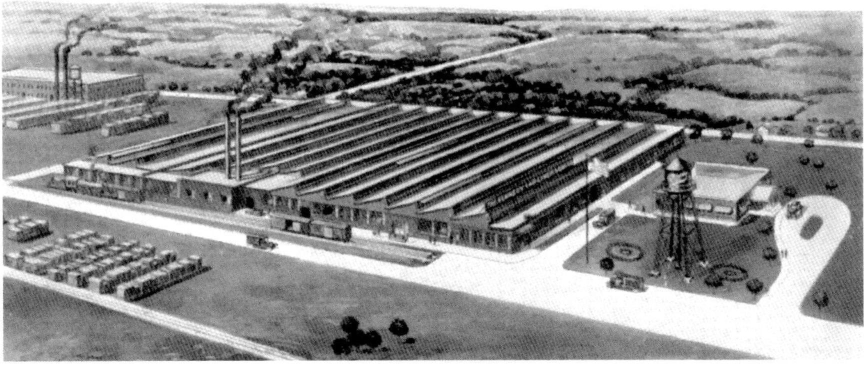

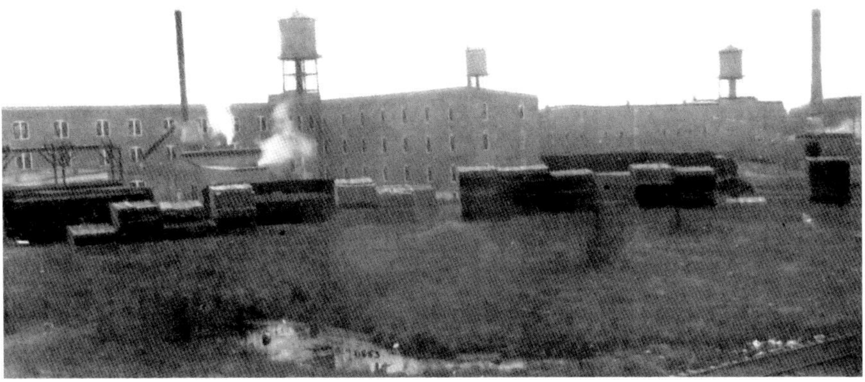

After the war years, Shelbyville was able to make repairs to its streets and sidewalks, as well as upgrades to the police and fire departments after years of sacrifice. Today, Shelbyville enjoys easy access to major interstate systems, up-to-date airport facilities and a good quality of life for all who call the city home. Those who relocate to Shelbyville find it to be a great place to raise their families in a variety of homes with gorgeous architecture. Entities such as the chamber of commerce and Mainstreet Shelbyville are dedicated to improving the town and the quality of life for its residents, one brick at a time.

"From the moment you enter Shelby County, you can see pride throughout the community," says the chamber of commerce website. "Whether your preferences sway toward the country lifestyle with acreage to spread your wings—or you enjoy walking to a city park from your downtown home, Shelbyville and Shelby County harmonize in ways its residents can attest to—and visitors appreciate."

"What makes this city unique is not only the many generations of families who still call this community home, but also Shelbyville has a lot more going on than most people know about, and we like it that way," Baumgartner said. "We are fortunate to live in a community that has a little bit of everything going for it."

Chapter 3

TRANSACTIONS AND TRANSPORTATION

The importance of the railroads and banks to Shelby County cannot be underestimated. As the community grew in the 1800s with more people settling in the area, it was only natural that the county government became more financially independent. This was greatly enhanced by the presence of financial institutions and the advent of the railroad systems.

Banks

McFadden wrote:

> *During the pioneering years, business had to be transacted for cash, or more commonly with bartered goods. Treasurers of public funds had to keep up the money on their own persons, which necessity probably was responsible for so much of the poor accounting. As Indianapolis was also young, merchants had to turn to Cincinnati and its river traffic for their goods and local produce had to be sold at the same market. Cash involved in these transactions was carried in saddlebags, the merchants frequently not only carrying money for their own business, but for that of their fellow townsmen as well.*

The first financial entity in the community was Elliot Hill & Co., established in 1851. Though little is known about this company, it was followed in 1855 by the Shelby Bank. The original operators of the company were John Elliot, James Hill and Samuel Hamilton. McFadden wrote that Alfred Major joined the company in 1857, but it was a poor economic time in the nation. Gold had been discovered in California, and though that led to a tremendous boom period, there was a backlash. Many western banks failed, and some other financial centers were forced to close their doors. Thanks to the faith of its owners, the Shelby Bank was able to continue operations.

In 1892, Hamilton died and the bank had to undergo a period of reconstruction. The result was the Shelby National Bank. Hamilton's original partners had reorganized in 1859 and became Elliot and Major Co., which offered residents two banks to serve their needs. Eventually, Elliot and Major sold their bank to John Blessing and two other men, who restructured the institution in 1865 as the First National Bank. "The following month the newspapers carried the notice that it had been authorized by the Controller of the Treasury to do business under that name," McFadden quoted. "In 1869 it increased its capitalization, Alfred Major buying the new stock and at that time John Elliot became President and A.D. Lynch, cashier." It would remain in existence until the Great Depression forced the bank to close its doors.

Railroads, the Cash Cows

There had been some experimentation with railroads in the 1830s, but by the 1850s rail lines and Shelby County would create a lasting marriage. The first railroad in Indiana, and west of the Alleghany Mountains, was the Lawrenceburg & Indianapolis Railroad. Promoted by Shelbyville judge William J. Peaslee, the 1¼-mile oak rail track was built in 1834 from Shelbyville to Lewis Creek and had a single horse-drawn one-coach train. Although it helped to calm the fears of rail travel, the line was abandoned after a few years when no investors could be found to extend the line to Indianapolis. Indiana's first steam railroad, the Madison & Indianapolis (M&I), was built in 1847, and the Shelbyville Lateral of the M&I was opened in 1850 running the 16 miles from Edinburgh to Shelbyville. Two other branch lines, the Knightstown & Shelbyville and the Shelbyville & Rushville, also opened in 1850. These lines through Shelby County created enough traffic in the community that Henry Irish constructed a building that would be used as a hotel to accommodate rail travelers. Throughout

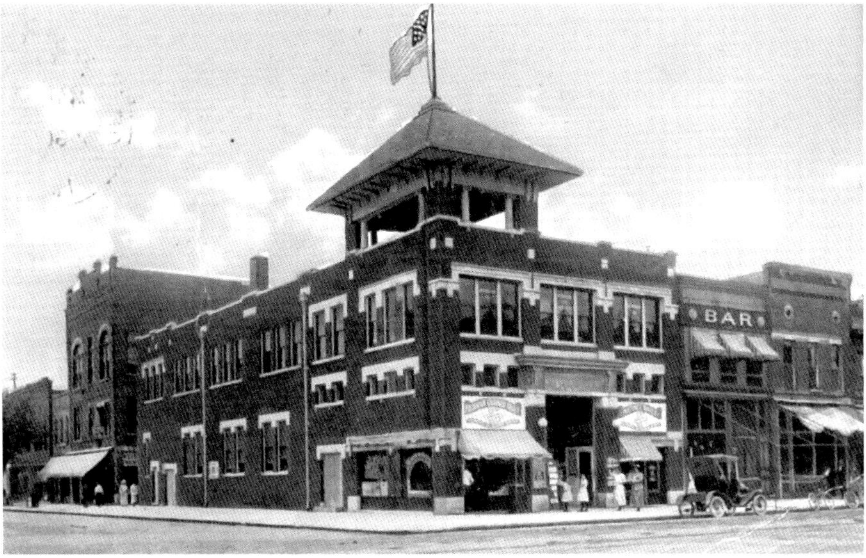

A postcard of the Alhambra building in the center of Shelbyville. The previous building on this site was used as a hotel for railroad travelers.

the years, this building was used for a variety of purposes until it was razed to make way for the Alhambra building.

Built for $200,000, the Knightstown & Shelbyville Railroad folded faster than any other line in the state's history. This was partially due to an engine explosion early on, but the line also had many operational issues. John Harper, author of several biographical sketches of the region, said that the original engine was nearly the same size as the old-time steam traction engine with very large drive wheels. "It is said that on the first excursion from Knightstown to Shelbyville they accommodated the passengers by placing seats cross-wire on flat cars and when the engine stalled on a grade, the passengers would all get off and help push." In addition, the train had to stop many times in order to move livestock off the track.

With only one boxcar, two passenger cars and an engine, the train's maximum speed was fifteen miles per hour (the average for the time was ten miles per hour). It was not uncommon for passengers to run alongside the train and jump aboard. Local legends such as this were commonplace. One persistent story maintains that an old lady in the community became so angry with the railroad company for killing her pig that she greased the rails with lard and put the train out of commission.

"Stations were maintained at Knightstown, Carthage, Morristown, Hanover and Shelbyville…The Morristown station stood on the site of

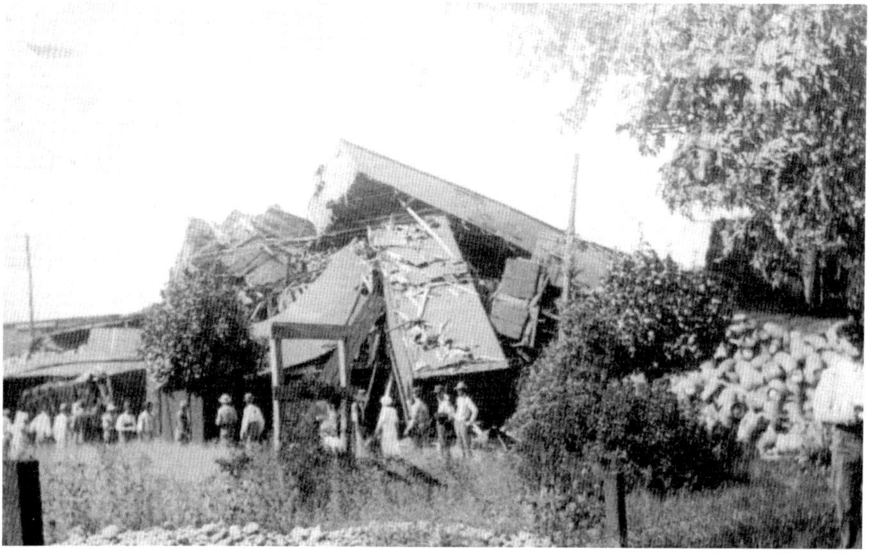

Train wrecks such as these were common in the early days of the rail lines, which sometimes crippled the company's ability to maintain the railroad for very long. *Courtesy of Virginia Williams.*

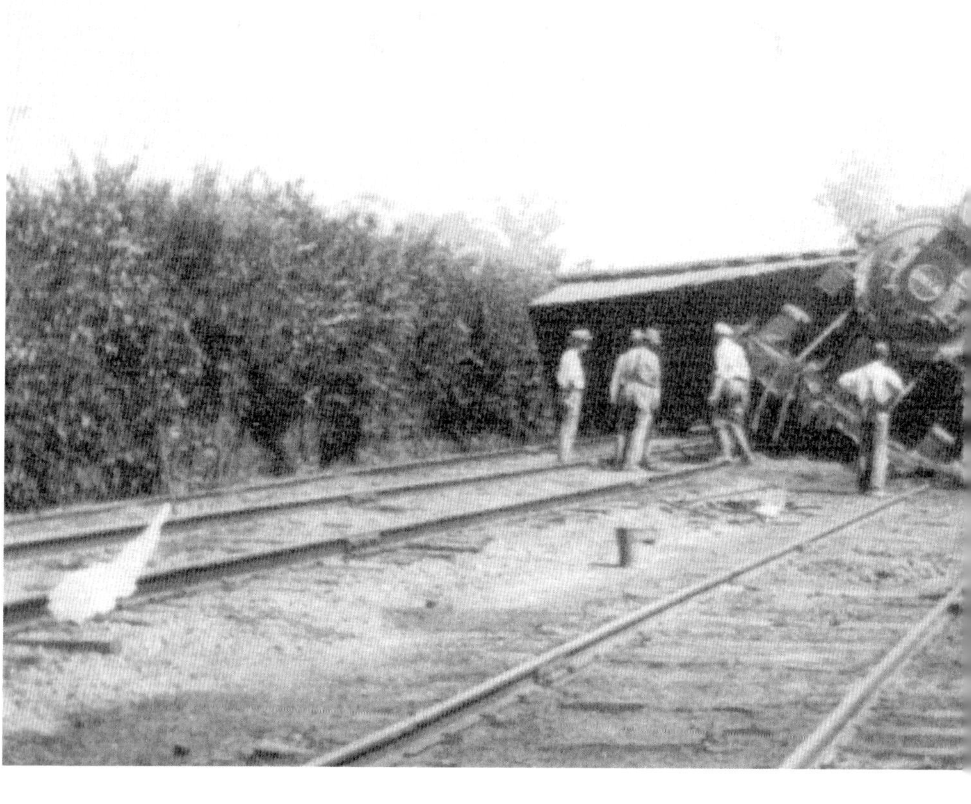

the Methodist parsonage," wrote Harper. "The tracks ran through the alley west of the Kopper Kettle which at the time was a large two-story grain warehouse."

McFadden noted that the stories surrounding that early line were nothing short of legendary and included the "proverbial story of the dog who bade his master farewell when the latter boarded the train at Carthage and the dog was wagging his tail in greeting at the Shelbyville Depot when his master arrived."

In 1858, there was a meeting held in order to entertain the idea of rebuilding the railroad due to its poor condition. New stockholders, as well as new rails, were installed, and the new railway lasted until 1863, at which time the scrap rails and iron were used for military needs during the Civil War.

Florence Rock's memoirs include a story of her father earning the contract to build the new depot in Morristown for the "new" railroad that was under construction in 1867. It would eventually be known as the Junction Railroad and was designed to extend from Hamilton, Ohio, to Indianapolis. Rock's

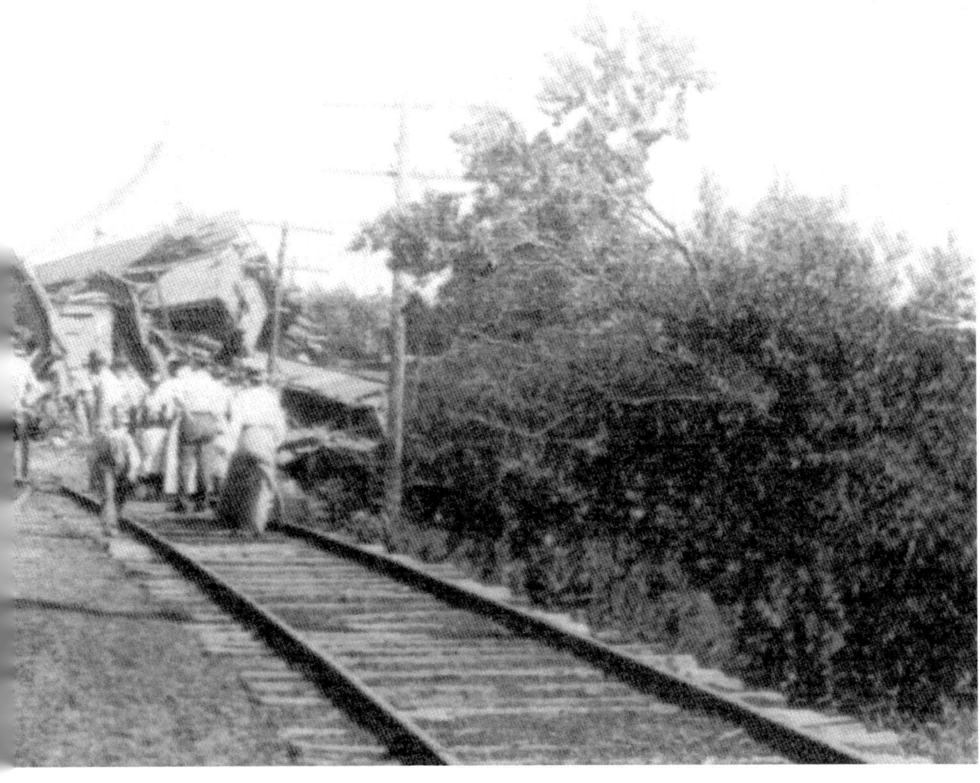

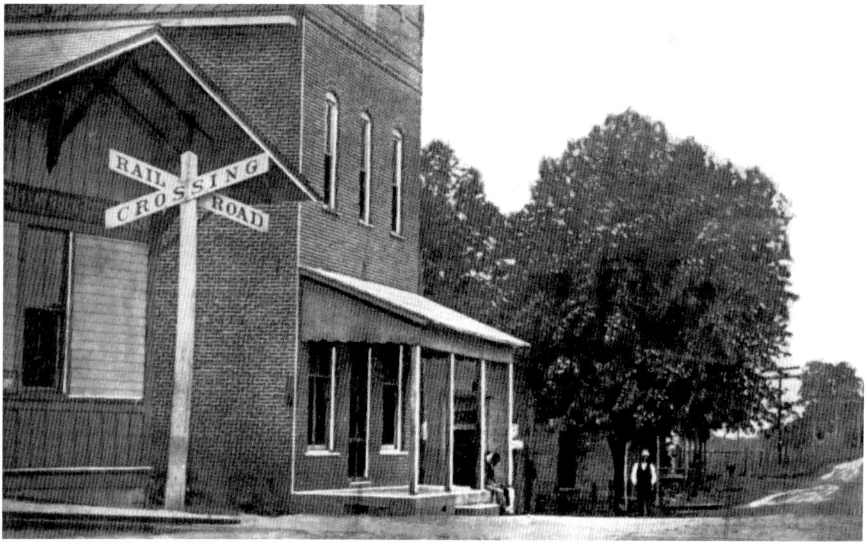

The business portion of Flat Rock, Indiana, showing how rail traffic was a staple within the community.

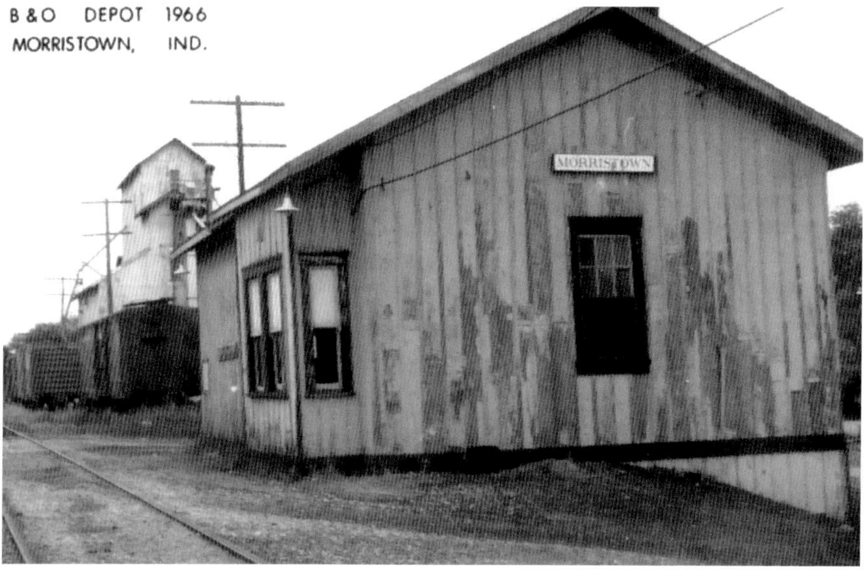

The B&O Depot in Morristown in 1966. Today, CSX is still traveling through the county and celebrating its B&O heritage.

grandfather, Jonathon Johnson, owned the land that was used as the right of way, as well as the gravel pits and the depot. He sold the property for seventy-five dollars an acre in January of that year. When the railroad was completed, it was operated by Samuel Mitchell and Billy Burns, who boarded at Rock's house.

"The labor of roadbed building was nearly all done by hand and wheelbarrow and then by gravel train," Rock wrote, noting that more than two hundred Chinese laborers were involved in the construction of the railroad. "They were camped at the gravel pit west of town…people of the surrounding country would assemble on Sundays to observe the Chinese with their long queues, eating their rice with chopsticks."

The next road to make a name for itself was the Shelbyville & Rushville. It was twenty miles long and connected with the other roads in the M&I system. Apparently, this road was nearly as bad as the Knightstown & Shelbyville. One passenger said that while no one had ever been killed on the road, it was more likely that someone would starve to death trying to get anywhere considering the trip might take anywhere from a few hours to several days.

The Jeffersonville & Indianapolis Railroad in 1852 proved to be the line that caused controversy in the county. McFadden said that line ran from Columbus and met up with the M&I, but the problem occurred when both lines had a set of tracks that ran "side by side to Edinburgh." The M&I felt there should be a compromise and authorized the J&I Railroad to use its tracks to get to Indianapolis. "Gradually, the Jeffersonville gained control of the Madison, although actual consolidation did not take place until 1866. It then became known as the J.M. and I.," wrote McFadden.

McFadden wrote that in 1871, the Pennsylvania Railroad bought the JM&I, and passenger travel remained available on the line until 1922. For the next eight years, the trains carried both passengers and cargo until the passenger service was dropped and it became strictly a freight service.

The Lawrenceburg & Indianapolis Railroad, which had honored the county as the site of its early rail experiment, became the Lawrenceburg & Upper Mississippi Railroad in 1850. It eventually completed plans to have a road that ran from Indianapolis through Shelbyville to Cincinnati, and in 1853, the railroad became the Indianapolis & Cincinnati Railroad.

"The I. and C. passed through many vicissitudes, merged with other short roads, which formed a direct line to Chicago and in Shelby County a branch line was built from Fairland to Franklin to Martinsville. In 1880 it became part of the Big Four system and finally, in 1930 the New York Central," wrote McFadden.

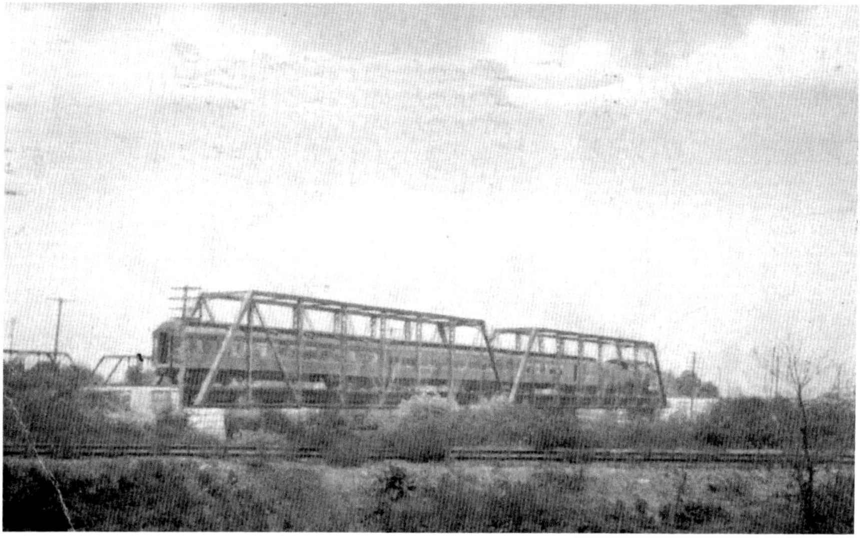

The various trains that moved through the community merged to become part of the Big Four System in 1880. This postcard shows one of the Big Four trains crossing the Blue River.

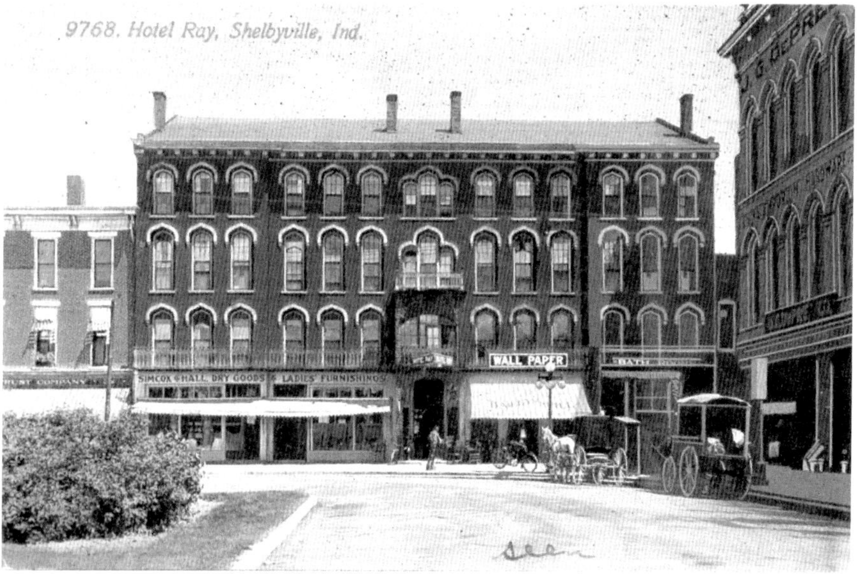

Above and opposite: These vintage postcards illustrate the businesses and hotels that cropped up along the Public Square about the same time that rail travel began to make its mark in the community.

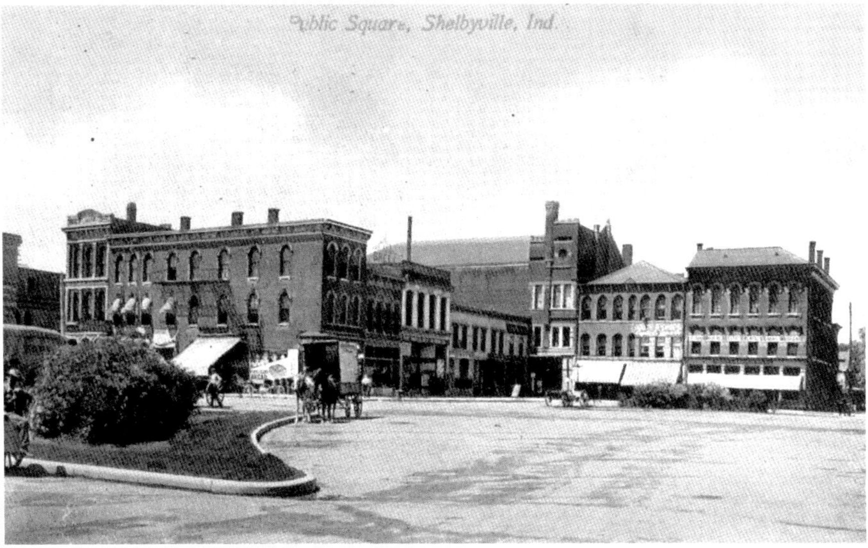

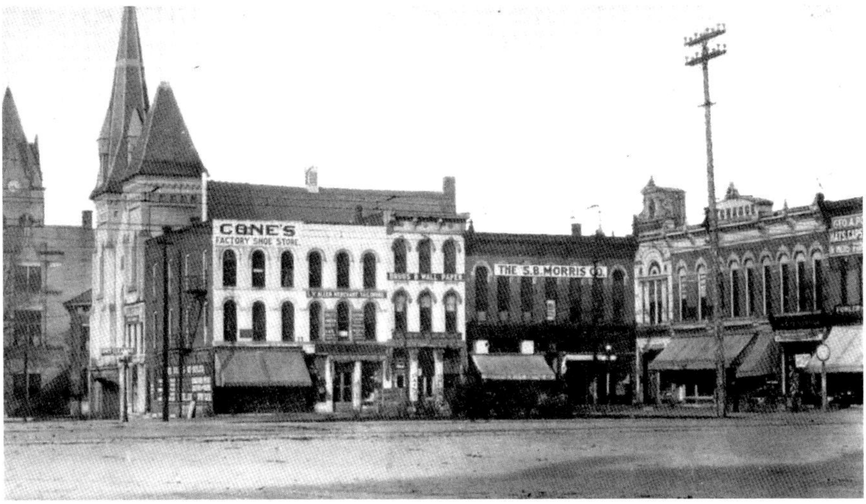

The railroad history in the community remains a confusing one. Competition between various entities was fierce. As various early roads became defunct, there was often a great deal of litigation aimed at the railroad companies that were able to survive. It was easily a question of survival of the fittest. The bigger railroads often crushed the smaller competitors, putting them out of business entirely.

With the onset of travelers and the shipment of goods, newer and bigger buildings were constructed throughout town. Some were used as hotels, taverns and public houses, while others were retail storefronts. The Public Square became the centralized hub for commerce in the area thanks to the early enthusiasm that brought rail travel to the state. To this day, it remains a bustling intersection with a number of businesses and shops that have become destinations for the Shelby County community.

The Interurban

Another form of mass transportation was the interurban. Known as traction cars, this electric car system was operated by a 3,300-volt mechanism strung over the track. Indiana was known for these entities and had more lines than any other state in the nation, according to Shelby County's history published by the Shelby County Historical Society. The original cars were wooden, but that eventually changed over time to cars made from steel. Interurbans operated at high speeds, and the line through Shelby County facilitated a rapid movement of people and goods into and out of the county several times a day.

"We rode them all the time," said Mary Buchanan. "The interurban cars were great!"

The interurban line arrived in the county about 1902. A round-trip fare on the car ran about seventy-five cents, and a trip to Indianapolis usually lasted about one hour. The interurban enabled people to move about for shopping, movies or other necessities for a fare that was cheaper than the railroads.

For the most part, the interurban cars had regular stops unless it was an express car that didn't have a stop between destinations. Some of the local cars could be boarded at any intersection along the tracks. Farmers used the cars to transport their large milk cans, and some cattle cars were attached to the passenger cars in order to expedite transportation to markets. At places like Boggstown and other communities, livestock pens were erected near the interurban stops.

"The Motorman in front manned the controls and reached out a window over the front mounted steel 'cow catcher' with a long metal pole to switch tracks especially when following the trolley lines in Indianapolis," read *Shelby County, Indiana History and Families*. In addition, there was a conductor on the back collecting fares and assisting riders as they embarked and departed.

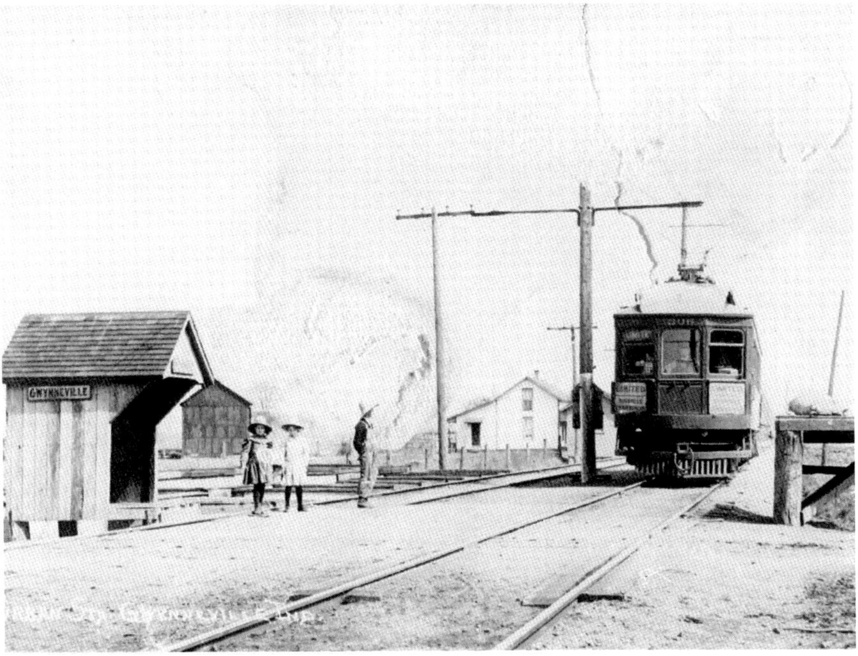

The interurban was another popular form of mass transit. *Courtesy of Donna Tracy at the Blue Bird Restaurant.*

Stores and factories began to depend on the line as a way to get small items delivered in a timely fashion. Automobiles also had to give the interurbans an extra-wide berth after noticing the number of fender benders caused by the cars. While there were a few deaths caused by the interurbans, they were very successful modes of transportation. However, in 1932, the ride had come to the end of the line, and interurbans faded into history.

Chapter 4

JACKET COUNTRY

The sign along U.S. 52 near Blue River bears an ominous warning to travelers heading east: "You are now entering Jacket Country!" Despite the implied danger, the notice is only meant as a spirited intimidation to foes of the Morristown High School Yellow Jackets. The community itself is a docile throwback to a slice of Americana, where neighbors stop by to visit with one another, church congregations thrive and patriotism is worn with pride. It is also the kind of place where the local watering holes are the best spots to catch up on all the news around town.

Morristown's history began in 1820 with an influx of pioneer settlers who were opposed to slavery and also deeply committed to the education and religious training of their children. Original inhabitants of the area included James Hewitt and Firman Smith, who squatted just east of Blue River, along with Michael McCord, who built a cabin at the foot of the hill in what is now Morristown.

The town itself was incorporated that year, though it wasn't laid out until eight years later, when Samuel Morrison, Colonel Rezin Davis and Matthew Gosney (who acted as surveyor) created the 48 lots measuring 60 by 120 feet. Today, Morristown has 444 housing units to accommodate more than 1,200 citizens.

John E. Harper's historical sketch of Morristown's early years noted that early settlers all lived in log cabins, with the first frame houses not showing up until about 1840. The first mill was erected in Freeport in 1823 by Ira Bailey, and there were two schoolhouses in the area that also

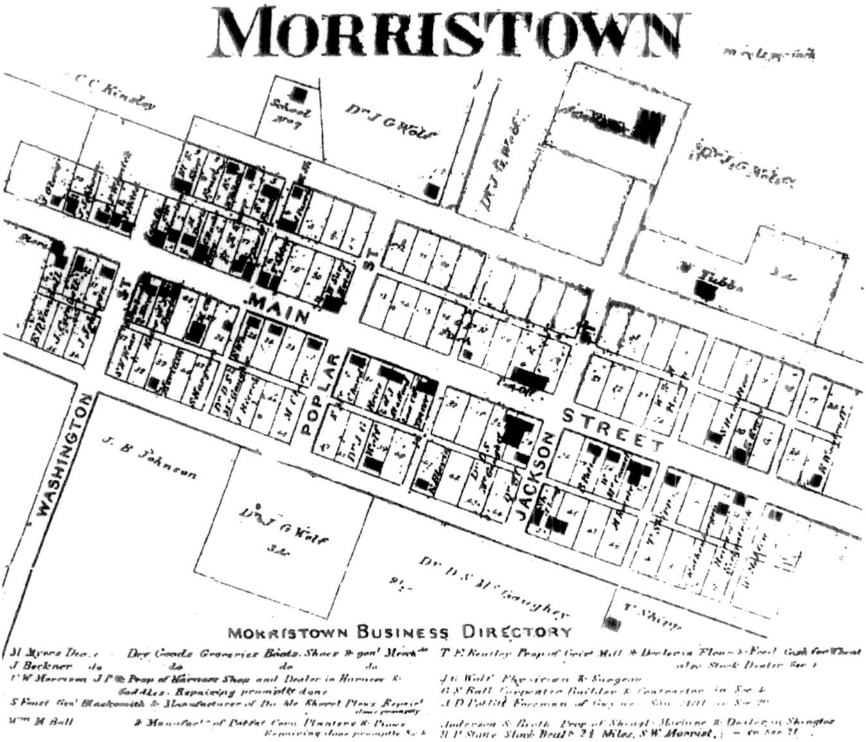

The initial plat of Morristown when it was originally founded, circa 1820. *Courtesy of Elaine Gobble.*

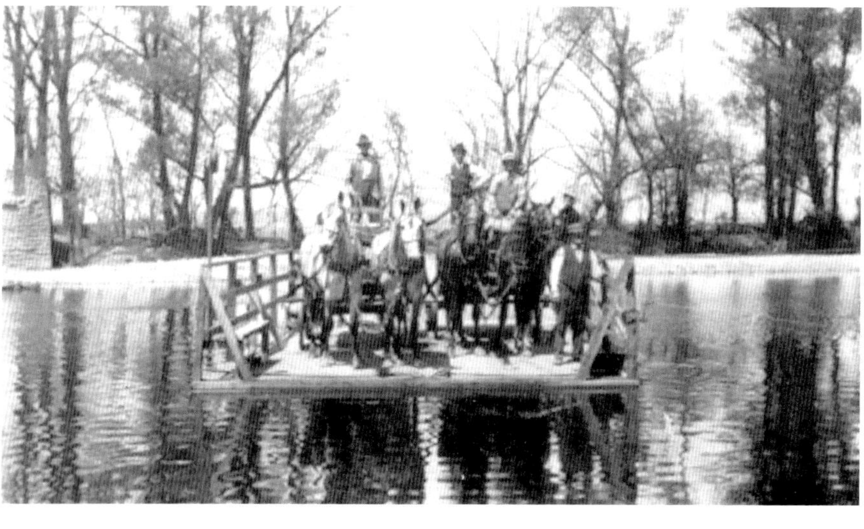

The Blue River Ferry near Morristown. Though this postcard was taken in 1913 during the Great Flood, it shows some of the early travel endured by settlers. *Courtesy of Virginia Williams.*

served as church buildings. The first denomination to be established in the community was a Methodist class that was organized in 1822 by Jonathon Johnson and his wife. Services were originally held in their home but were eventually moved to the Old Union School building, where services were held until 1839. Other congregations included a Baptist class and a Christian denomination by the end of the 1840s.

When it comes to shedding some light on Morristown's early years, one need look no further than the 1946 published memoirs of Florence Johnson Rock. Rock was born on August 8, 1850, in her maternal grandfather's home, which was also an inn. The home was located on the old J.K. Kemper homesite. Rock was the oldest of four children born to Samuel Johnson and Zelda Spurrier. Her extensive memory includes an incident in which a group of clock peddlers kidnapped some local girls. "They kidnapped Kate Davis and her sister…a posse was quickly organized and went after the peddlers and brought them back with the girls…The citizens destroyed their wagon and the clocks then assisted them from the community for keeps," she wrote.

Rock's education began at her mother's knee when she was quite young. Zelda taught her children the alphabet by cutting out large letters from the *Cincinnati Gazette*. Rock also credited her father with being her main teacher, as she often accompanied him to the schools he taught in, but her formal schooling began at the Old Union School under the tutelage of Miss Delilah Cottingham, who boarded with the family while she taught at the cabin school. "The schoolhouse was a log building heated by a fireplace. The seats and desks were puncheons. Old Union was the only log schoolhouse I attended, as by the time I was ready for school most of the buildings were frame."

Rock's memoirs serve as a look back at an idyllic time when she traveled with her family by horse and wagon to the state fair in Indianapolis, rode on the Knightstown Railroad before it folded and gathered the mail from Rebecca Gadd, who served as the postmistress, sorting letters for Morristown citizens after the post was brought from Shelbyville by David Clary on horseback.

Clary and his sister Margaret lived in a small cottage while he operated the mail run to Morristown, Freeport, Hanover and Marion. He was also a stagecoach driver who traveled in all kinds of weather. According to Harper, he had a long black beard, a short-stemmed pipe and very strong breath. "His sister was not so even tempered as her brother. She objected to the boys sliding down the hill past her house and she enforced her objections with hot water, hot ashes and a hot flow of language," Harper wrote.

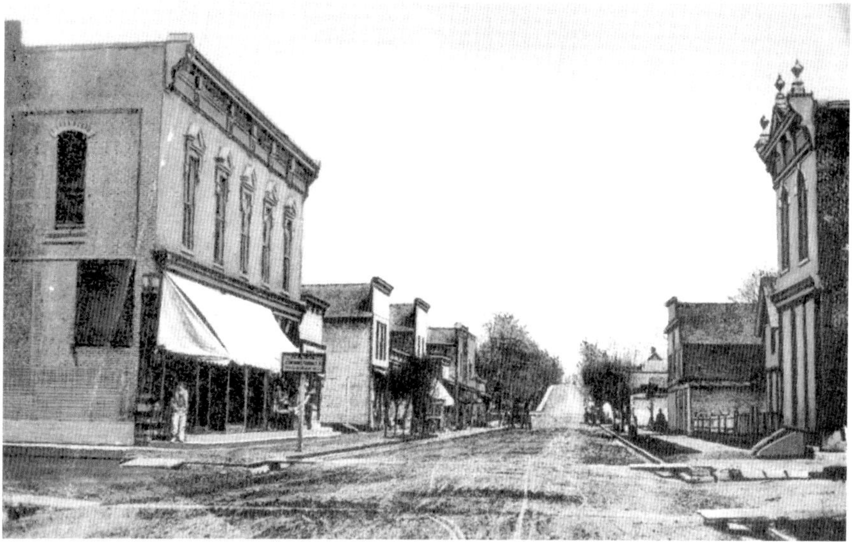

A vintage postcard depicting a street scene in Morristown, a quaint community with American charm. Some of the families in the community have been here for generations.

Despite their odd temperament, the family was kindhearted and ended up leaving their land to the town after they died. Gadd lived on the hill along with many of the other prominent people in Morristown (many of whom were given titles of endearment by Rock) who made their homes near the commercial district of the community.

"The stores were very small and the stock was limited. We produced nearly everything we needed on our farms. We no longer spun our own cloth, but we did produce our own food," Rock wrote.

The Singing Schools

Rock eventually attended school at Old Seminary on the Hill. During her time there, she also participated in lyceums every month, in which students recited various pieces with Adelia Roerty Shipp serving as organist for the entertainment. In addition, parents had the opportunity to participate in the singing school. In 1835, Dr. David S. McGaughey, who was not only a physician but also a musician, organized a young people's singing class.

Rock reports that the singing school used the Missouri Harmony book as its guide, and what started out as an adult group eventually led to the children forming their own group as well. In fact, her grandfather was the song leader for the children's class. With no instruments to guide them, Mr. Johnson would hold a tuning fork to his ear in order to achieve the pitch he needed.

"He would announce the number chosen and tell whether it was a long meter or a short meter and would then read a couple of lines. Then the congregation would sing those. He would then read a couple more which they would sing…I can still see my grandfather as he read out, 'How tedious and tasteless the hours when Jesus no longer I see.'"

Harper wrote that the interest in the singing schools eventually led to the building of Asbury Chapel, which was constructed with timber from the grounds and contained two entrances, one for men and one for women. The late 1830s would also see the beginning of Asbury Cemetery. The first burial in the cemetery was of a stagecoach driver who patronized Rock's grandfather's inn and slept too close to the fire (no one ever knew the man's name). Over time, the cemetery gained a considerable reputation as within its precincts lie many pioneers, a soldier from the War of 1812, two soldiers from the Mexican War, fifty soldiers from the Civil War, a few who served in the Spanish-American War, veterans of both World Wars, as well as others who served in various conflicts in the latter portion of the twentieth century. Today, Asbury Cemetery has a section dedicated to honoring veterans where annual Memorial Day exercises occur.

Although the singing classes were very popular, eventually the demand of raising families and the hardships of pioneer life led them to disband. They were succeeded by the Diapason Class in 1861. Stephen W. Dugan of Johnson County, who played the violin, taught the class and offered the community a chance to come and learn music. Rock said:

> *The class was lots of fun. We met every night for about two weeks, then we had a big Christmas concert and then Professor Dugan came back after the holidays and the class met every two weeks…The leader directed with his violin, playing the different parts and helping out the basses, tenors, sopranos or altos wherever they got stuck on the notes. On the blackboard he explained the round note system. He tested voices to see who could sing high and who could sing low and assigned them to the proper places.*

During the Civil War years, the singing classes suffered as everyone was too excited or sad to sing, and practice was held sporadically. But after the war, the singing classes reconvened and became bigger than ever. Rock recalled how the classes became so well known that invitations were received from Arlington and Rushville for the class to come and sing for those communities as well. "We always had a good time on those trips," she wrote.

A Growing Community

Businesses in Morristown grew as the community did. Initially, there was the gristmill located two miles north of town, but it burned down in 1885. There was no mortician in the town, so whenever there was a need for an undertaker someone had to be sent on horseback twelve miles to Shelbyville to fetch Mr. Cummins.

According to Rock, the first telegraph operator in the community was a man named Penrose Hughes from Hamilton, Ohio, who boarded with Rock's mother. She said the third operator was a man by the name of Daniel Shumway, but he was eventually replaced by the first female telegraph operator in the state, Ella Ross.

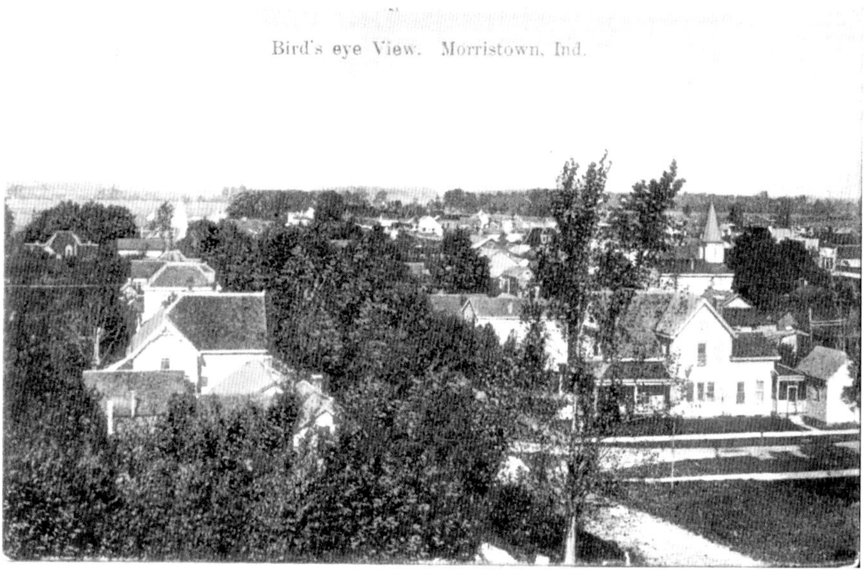

A bird's-eye view of Morristown from a vintage postcard showing a thriving community in a bustling county.

"The depot was also the local elevator," she remembered. "In the basement, a horse went round and round hitched to a long pole, to furnish the power to elevate the grain in buckets from the dump to the first floor or to the cars on the siding as required."

Of course, the early roads of Morristown were little more than trails themselves. As more and more settlers began to call the community home, the towns began laying logs over swampy areas of the trails, an improvement known as a "corduroy" road. Turnpikes followed, as did gravel roads, which were constructed by a stock company. The upkeep for the roads was paid for by a nominal toll charge that was implemented whenever someone wanted to cross in or out of town. Rock said she remembered one of the tollgates being located on the southeast corner of the property where the canning company would eventually be located before moving to the south side of the road. Rock said the gate was originally administered by Billy Wrenick but later operated by Silas McGrew. "Some of the young blades who did not like McGrew very well used to heat pennies red hot on the big barrel stove at the Joseph V. Shipps store and drive rapidly to the toll gate and dump the pennies into McGrew's hand."

She noted that two of the other tollgates were located at Hanover Road and Rangeline and were operated by women: Nancy Jane McConnell and Mrs. Sarah Middleton.

Freeport and Hanover

Morristown wasn't the only booming community in those early days. The village of Freeport and the town of Hanover were popular settlements as well, according to Harper. Freeport got its start in 1823, when Ira Bailey built the first mill from timbers that were hewn by hand. He also operated a general store, making long trips to New York in order to bring merchandise back to the settlers. While he was away, his wife would sleep during the hours that the mill was running and then stand guard over the property, as there were still many Indians in the area.

Freeport was known as the home of Louis Bailey, a famous inventor and son of Ira Bailey. Harper wrote that Bailey is known for making the first working model of the Gatling gun (machine gun). "It consisted of a cluster of barrels revolved by a crank, and loaded and fired once each during a revolution of the group," he said.

"I heard a rumor that somewhere in a bank vault, the original gun still exists," said Don Baumgartner. "Now, I don't know if that is true or not, but the legend of that gun has been circulating for years."

Another of Bailey's inventions was a weapon consisting of a single-barrel gun with cartridges that were fastened to a web belt. Bailey also made the first machine that corrugated a stovepipe, as well as perfecting some farming equipment. In spite of his ingenuity, his inventions didn't make him a wealthy man. Still, many of the vintage hardware catalogues of the time carried "Bailey" tools.

Freeport became a religious community in 1832–33 when missionaries Peter Clinger and Hawkeye arrived to help organize the first church. Meetings were originally held in settlers' homes, but eventually the first proper church, the M.P. Church of Freeport, was formed in 1866. Another entity in the area was a large two-story building located on the west side of Freeport that was the home of the early stores owned by merchants John Corell and John McCormack. Harper said that dances were often held on the second floor of the building as well.

The town of Hanover is all but a memory for those who remember the community when it was something of a rival to Morristown in the early days. Hanover was settled by folks from New England about 1820, with the first church congregation and school following in 1823. Mrs. Amaret Pollitt Logan offered her memories of those early days in Hanover:

> *There was the period when the Indian, once blood-thirsty and revengeful had become friendly. When they passed through the country and had to stop at a farm and ask a favor, the mother would lean the board upon which her baby was strapped against the fence while she did her errand… the howl of the wolf could be heard at night and the most pitiful cry of the panther, which for an instant one thought must be the cry of a lost child. These were lonely times for the mothers as the fathers were compelled to ride far for the necessities of life, and they could not make the trips between daylight and dark.*

Logan said that her mother was among the initial members of the Hanover church, which was presided over by Judge Cole, who studied the Bible, was very familiar with the scriptures and was quick to tell any preacher if he was wrong when it came to quoting the Bible.

"Later there was a Sunday School at Hanover and the people came from all over on horseback, two-horse wagons and barefoot. On a bright Sunday morning, children would start from home carrying their shoes and stockings under their arms," Logan wrote. "They would go barefooted until they came in sight of the church then they would put on their shoes and stockings and continue their journey."

The inn in Hanover was a major source of competition to Morristown's Davis Inn, and it was nothing for the owners of the two establishments to make the trip over to Arlington to remove each other's signboard in order to garner more customers for themselves. Harper said that in those early days Hanover possessed a sawmill, a blacksmith shop, a post office and several homes.

"Hanover was at one time a real town," wrote Logan. "There were within its borders a church, a schoolhouse, post office, blacksmith shop, one store with dry goods and groceries combined, and a steam saw mill with a great yard full of logs…there were two depots…and of course many houses and cottages."

Of course, the town of Hanover is no more, other than the cemetery that bears the marker memorializing the pioneers who settled the community, which was named for the town of Hanover, New Hampshire.

Blue River Park

During the 1880s, the Morristown vicinity was honored with another coup: the establishment of Blue River Park. The park was borne from an agreement with the Cincinnati, Hamilton & Dayton (CH&D) Railroad Company and Charles Muth, who leased a portion of his woods east of Blue River and north of the railroad tracks as a picnic grounds together with buildings such as a dining hall, recreation hall and dance hall. Coupled with the natural green space of the area, the park became a destination for Sunday school picnics, with congregations making the trip from Indianapolis and Cincinnati. "Almost every day a trainload of vacationers would unload on the platform…there was boating, swimming, games and other attractions for the various groups under the most favorable conditions," wrote Harper.

But there were other popular gatherings at Blue River Park, including "beer picnics," in which a baggage car would be loaded with beer kegs. Guests would bring dance bands and carry on with gambling activities, much to the chagrin of the Morristown people. Local law enforcement officials were kept quite busy when these gatherings took place, as they were

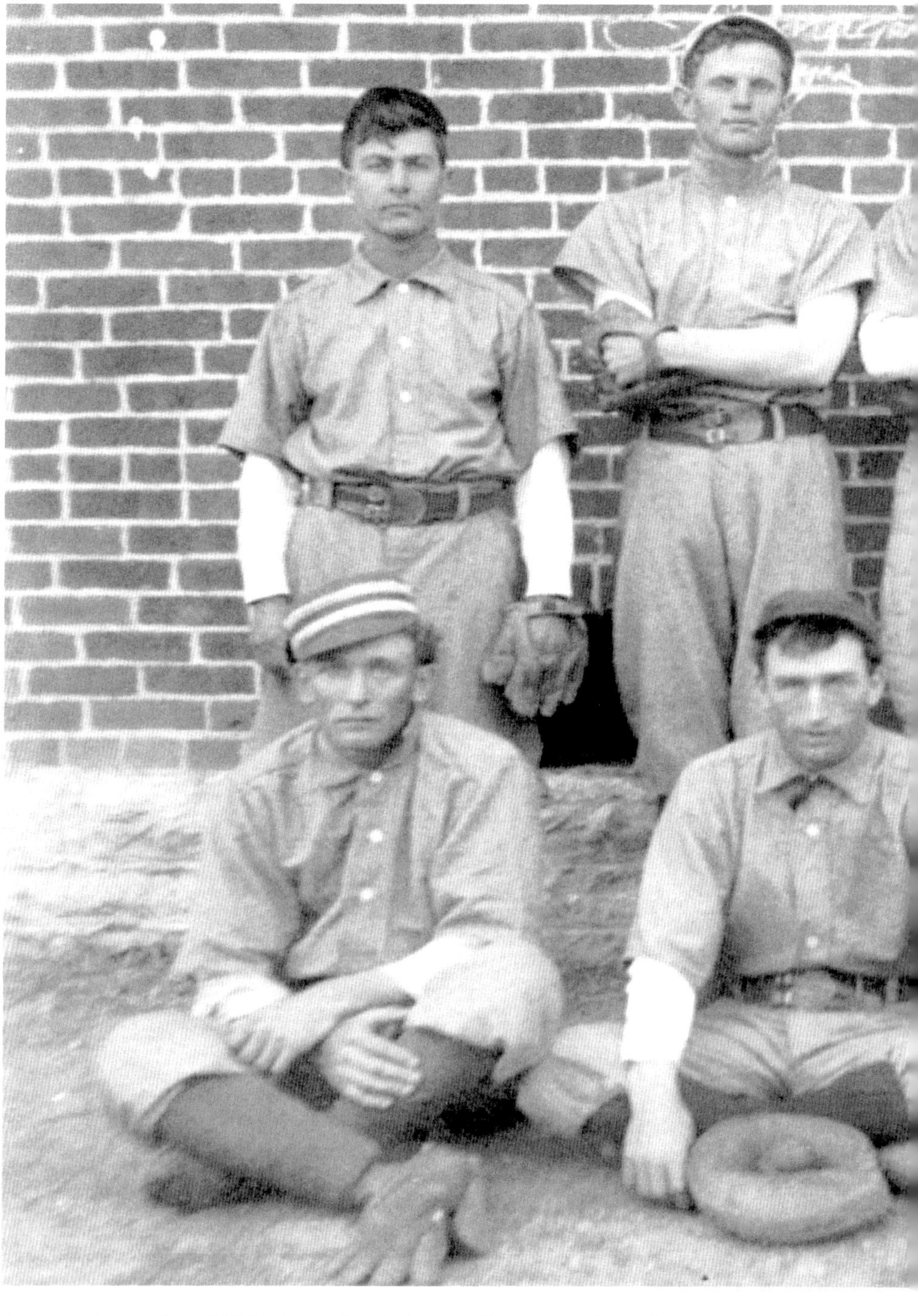

A vintage photo of an old Morristown baseball team. The community rallies behind its sports teams, and over the years, Morristown has been home to several well-respected

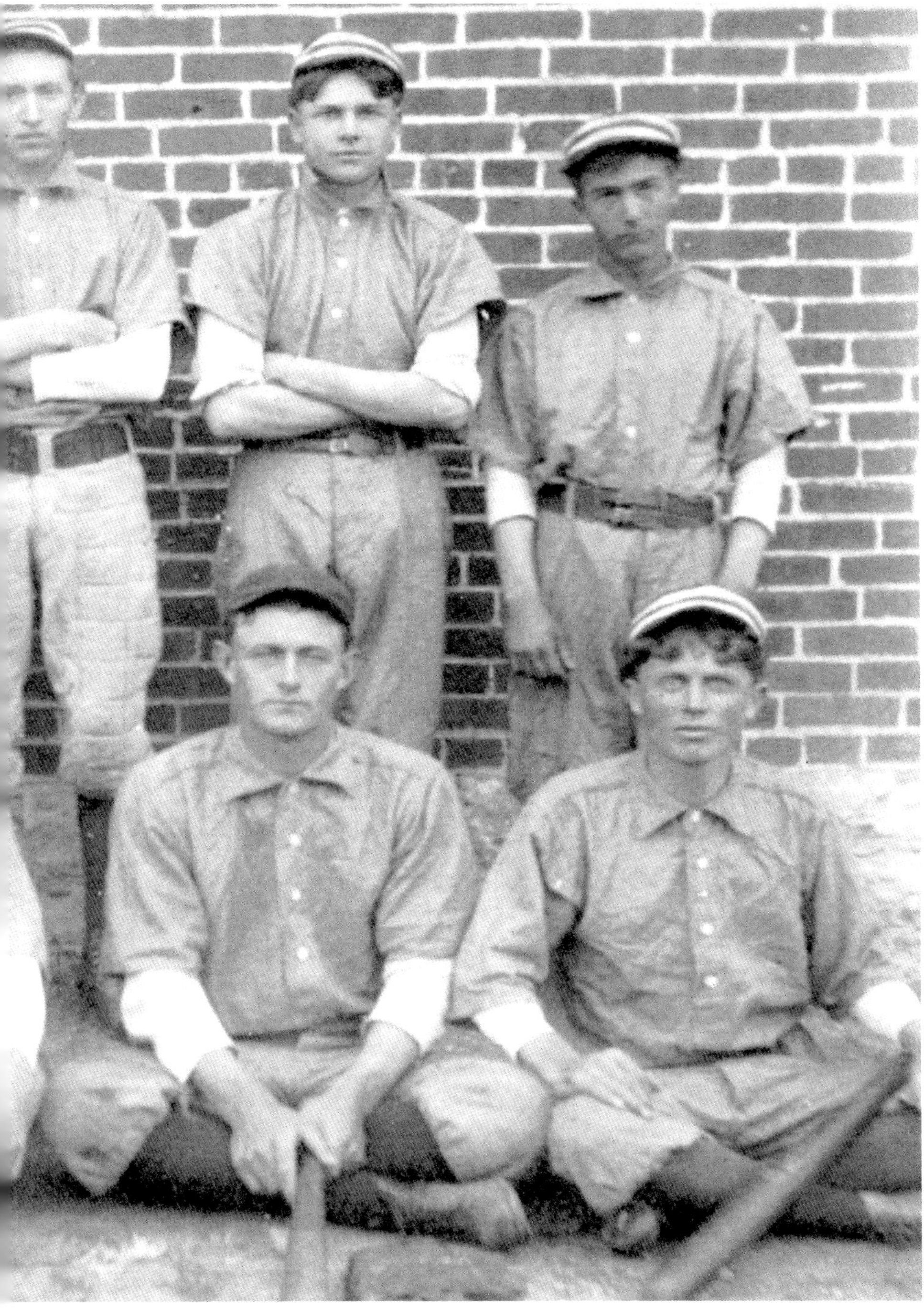

basketball teams, bowling leagues and a state championship volleyball team. *Courtesy of Donna Tracy at the Blue Bird Restaurant.*

the day a trainload of needy children were brought in for a day's outing. An inadequate amount of supervision allowed the youngsters to roam the town, Harper wrote. The resulting "tourism" could at times be difficult for the town.

Without a doubt, Morristown loves its sports teams. No matter if it's the local bowling league, a high school team or the community baseball club, the community rallies around its athletes and shows its support with a good turnout at every event.

Baseball may be the national pastime, but the game we know and love today didn't exist until after the Civil War. Harper explained that in the years between 1875 and 1925, it was as though every town and every community in the country had a championship team, and Morristown was no exception. "An old photo of the 'Rough and Ready' ball club was found among the effects of Frank Thatcher," he wrote. The photo was taken about 1880 and included early sportsmen such as John Huffman, W. Morrison, Dan Parsons and Henry G. (Dick) Wolf Jr., who is credited with having a fast arm and throwing the first curveball in the community.

"This team boasted two balls, five bats, a store bought mask and their fame as a ball club was known far and near," wrote Harper. "The first known diamond was in the old Wolf homestead just north of the community."

Town Treasures

The charm of Morristown is appealing to anyone who visits the community. Most people associate Morristown with one of its two world-class restaurants, the Bluebird or the Kopper Kettle.

The Kopper Kettle is a quaint, family-style restaurant with a rich history. As part of the Junction Railroad, which served the community from Shelbyville to Knightstown, the building was the farmers' grain elevator until the demise of the railroad. It was then converted into the Old Davis Tavern and was website, when Mr. Rogers died in 1885, the tavern was renamed and operated under the moniker the Valley House. The big porch and salesmen's sample room were added at this time, and according to its advertisement in the *Morristown Sun*, it contained thirteen well-ventilated rooms.

By the 1920s, ownership of the restaurant had passed to a Mrs. Robert (Muriel) Vredenburg. She longed to own and operate a tearoom and took a

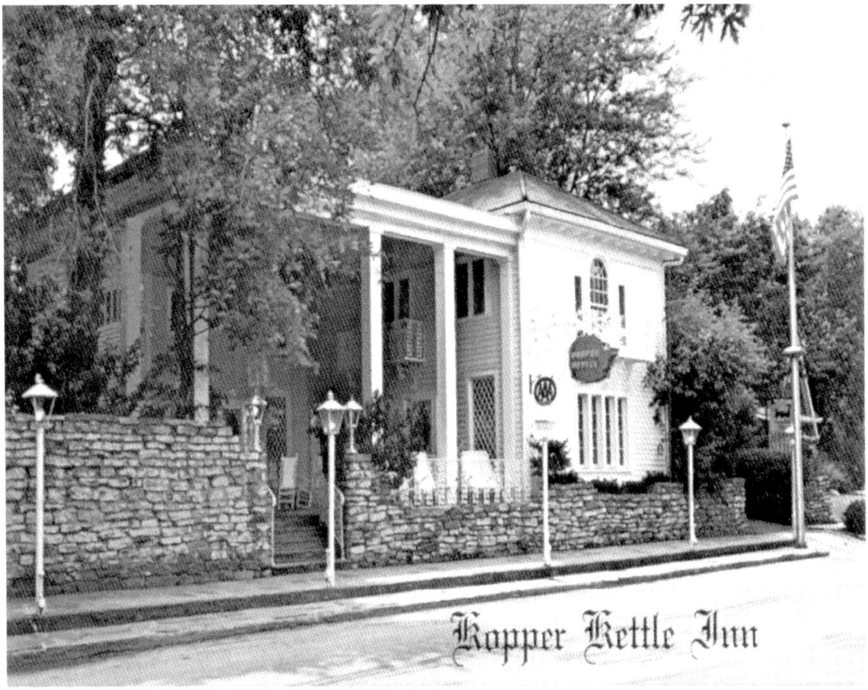

The Kopper Kettle Inn on U.S. 52 has been a staple in Morristown for many years. Known for its antique décor and family-style service, it is a one-of-a-kind dining experience.

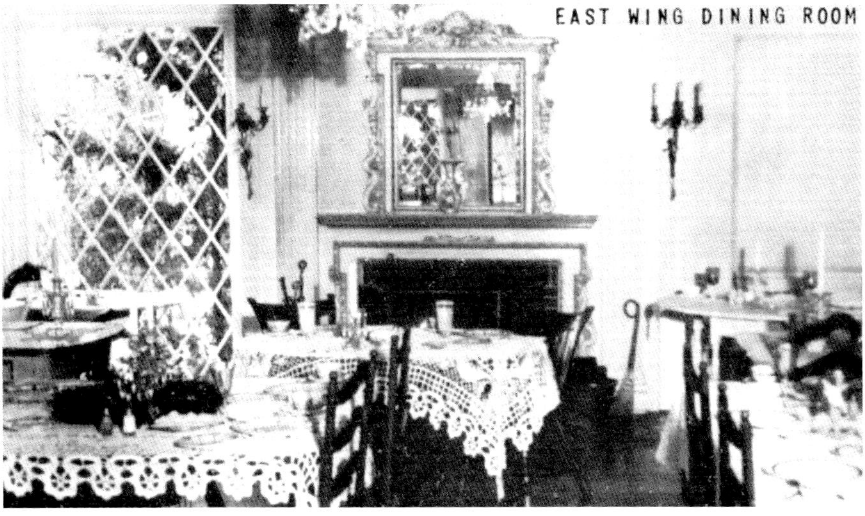

great passion in collecting antique copper tea kettles, which she hoped would draw patrons to her venture. She renamed the building the Kopper Kettle Inn and discontinued hotel operations.

Mrs. Vredenburg's tastes were not only limited to the tea kettles, but she also acquired many other antiques and treasures, including early American–, European- and Asian-influenced items that have remained part of the Kopper Kettle décor. Looking around the restaurant, it is obvious that nearly every piece of furniture is an antique.

"My sister got married in front of the fireplace at the Kopper Kettle," noted Mary (Toots) Buchanan, a longtime resident of Morristown. "It wasn't uncommon to hold a big event like that at the Kopper Kettle since it was such an elegant establishment."

Though Mrs. Vredenburg died in 1972, the reputation that had been generated by the Kopper Kettle remained when her daughter Mildred Taylor took over operations. She remained in charge until 1997, when Leigh and Kristi Langkabel joined the family and continued the tradition of history, ambiance and charm that is the Kopper Kettle Inn.

The Kopper Kettle has had a number of well-known guests, including James Whitcomb Riley, Charles Lindbergh, Herbert Hoover, Richard Lugar and Rosemary Clooney, not to mention the endorsement of Duncan Hines. Offering daily specials and family-style dinners, a meal at the Kopper Kettle is one experience you won't soon forget.

For a down-home meal served in a friendly atmosphere, the Blue Bird Restaurant is the place for a Sunday buffet or a cup of coffee with the locals. Specializing in fried chicken, the Blue Bird is the place to catch up on all the latest news around town.

The Blue Bird Restaurant came about in 1925, when Oscar and Zella Kinsey bought Johnson's Candy Shop and transformed the place into a restaurant that served the after-school crowd and casual diners. According to Shelby County's published history, Earl Webb won five dollars and the naming rights to the business, which is how it acquired the name "Blue Bird." In 1935, the Kinseys moved the restaurant to its current location on U.S. 52, and in 1937, when Mr. Kinsey died, the property was purchased by LaVern Nichols.

"It seems that I remember the Blue Bird being owned by Zella Kinsey," said Buchanan. "We had the Blue Bird, the Kopper Kettle and of course Mrs. Rock's café. There were a number of owners of the Blue Bird over the years, and I remember at one time, it had a dance floor and a nickelodeon that we enjoyed, but of course someone came along and said

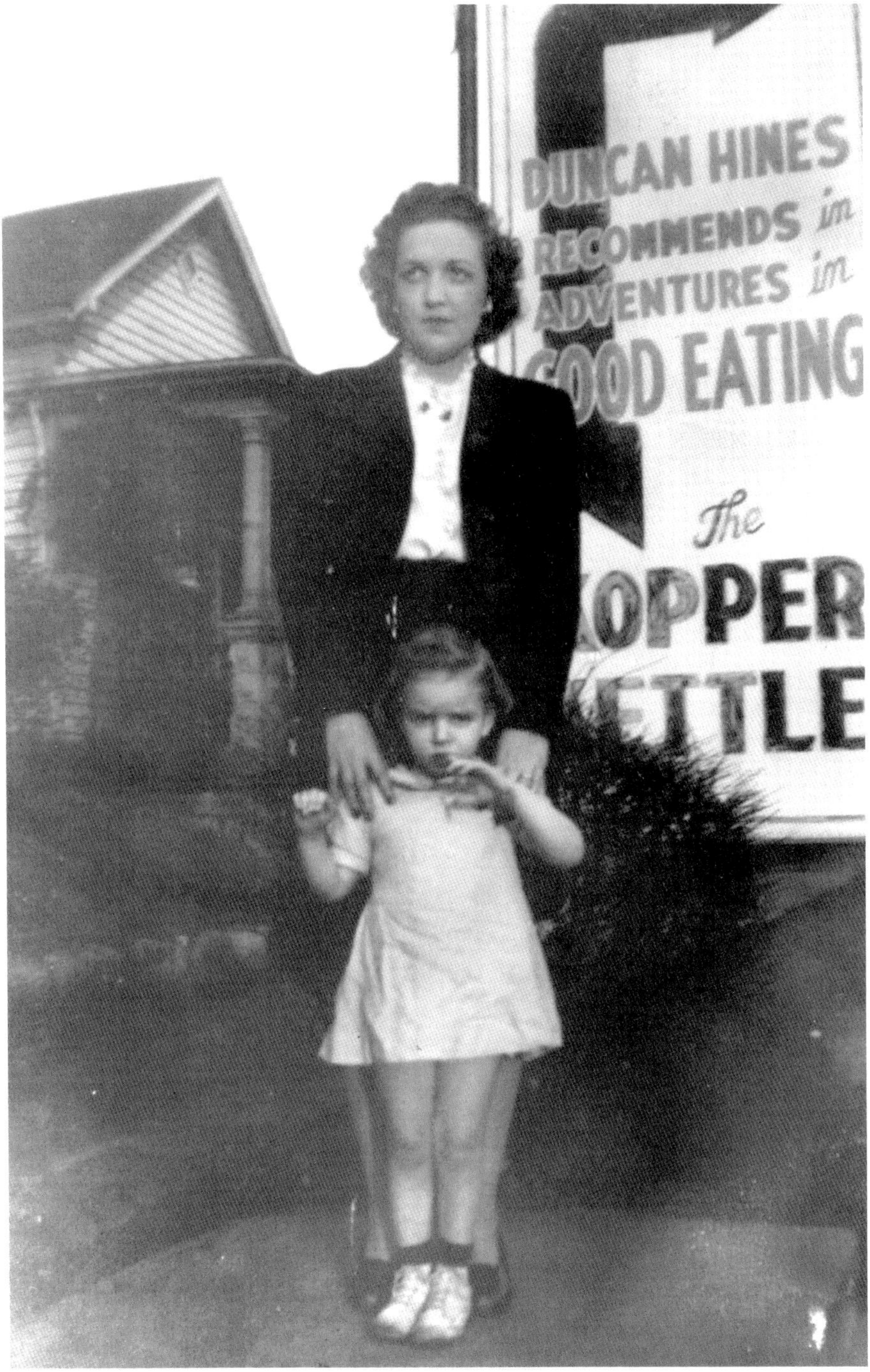

The Kopper Kettle was so popular that it even earned the endorsement of Duncan Hines, as shown in this photo of Mae Williams and Jackie Toon, circa 1945. *Author's private collection.*

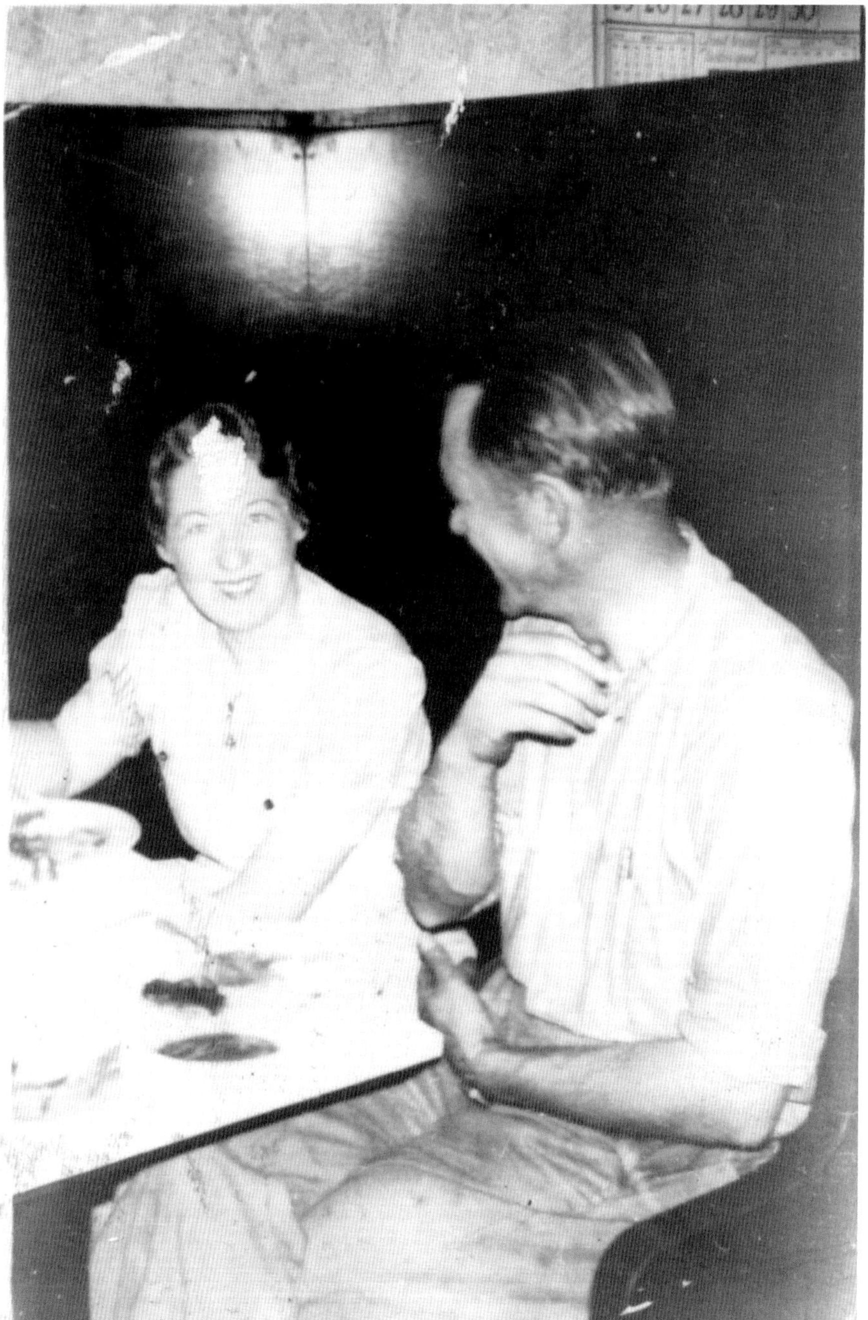

A Morristown couple enjoying a date at the Blue Bird Restaurant. Today, the establishment offers a coffee shop menu and a buffet that draws customers from all over the region. *Courtesy of Donna Tracy at the Blue Bird Restaurant.*

all that violated health rules or something and they took it away. It was fun while it lasted though."

Mrs. Kinsey did buy the restaurant back in time, as well as the store next door. Over the years, a number of people have owned the Blue Bird, and in the 1970s it became a cafeteria when Beryl Tracy purchased it.

Today, Donna Tracy is the proprietor and offers her guests a wonderful dining experience, with any number of folks traveling from throughout the

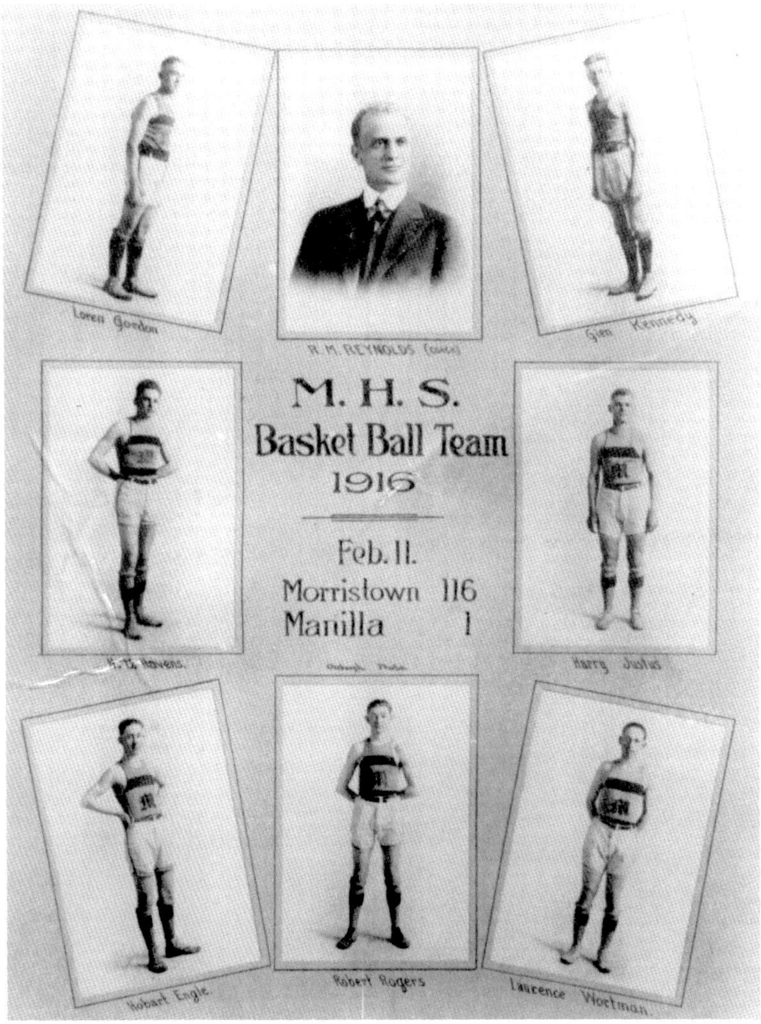

This page and next: These vintage sports shots hang in the Blue Bird Restaurant and show the evolution of Morristown's sports teams over the years. Basketball has always been a crowd-pleaser, but the Yellow Jacket state champion volleyball team has earned their respect in recent years as well. *Courtesy of Donna Tracy at the Blue Bird Restaurant.*

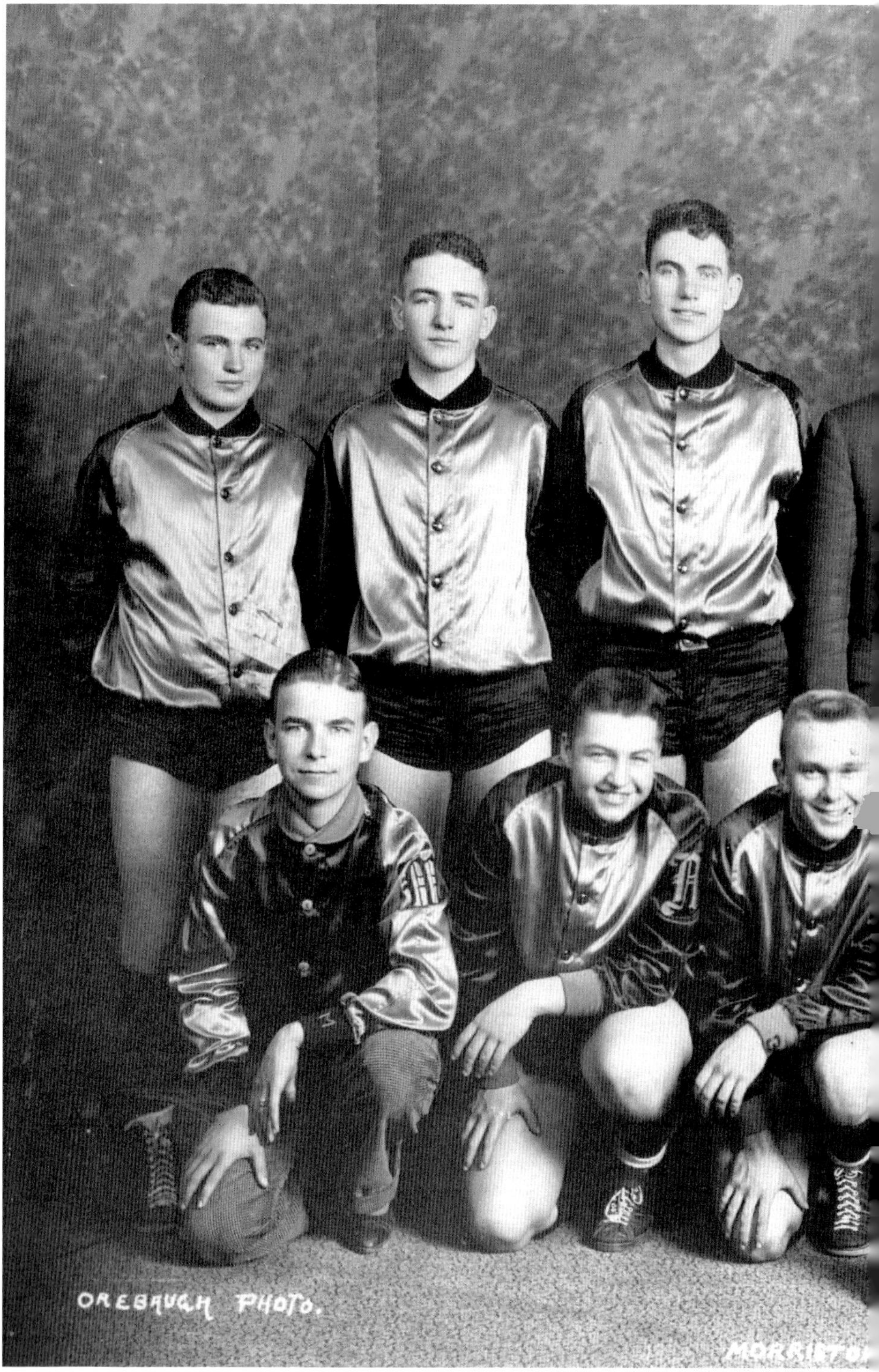
OREBAUGH PHOTO.

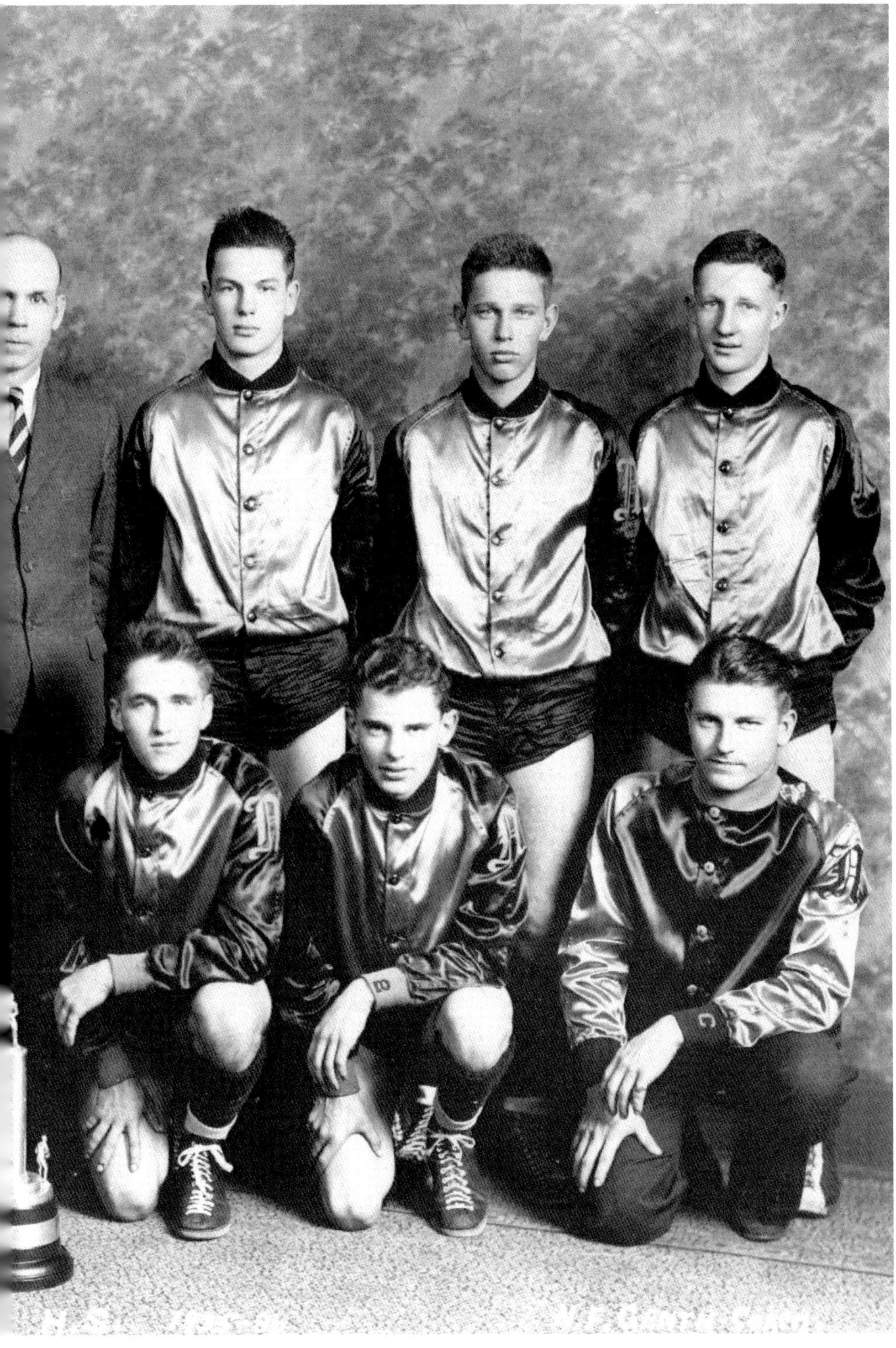

region to eat at the fried chicken buffet on the weekends. Locals are often found sitting at the round table in the coffee shop discussing current events or joking with the wait staff. It is the kind of restaurant that is a must-visit if you are traveling through Morristown and a place you can't wait to get back to once you have tasted the food!

Morristown's school system is also something the town is particularly proud of, and it isn't too hard to find plenty of fans with "Yellow Jacket pride." Morristown High School was established in 1922, with the first class graduating in 1924. Over the years, the building has undergone many remodelings, renovations and additions, including the 1937 addition of a gymnasium, cafeteria, shop and agricultural classrooms.

The high school was prominent enough to be invited to participate in the first state basketball championships long before every high school was entitled to play in the elimination format and before the class system of today's IHSAA sports. Morristown takes its teams very seriously, and it is not uncommon to see plenty of sports photos hanging around town. In fact, one of the community's great claims to fame is that Marvin Wood played for Morristown's 1943 basketball team before he went on to coach the legendary Milan 1954 state champs.

Difficult Days

Like other parts of the county, Morristown thought the 1920s were an era of prosperity and that the good times would last forever. However, the stock market crash and subsequent Depression severely affected the community as all around it jobs and salaries were cut and banks shut their doors for good.

"I don't remember too much about the Depression," said Virginia Williams, a longtime resident of Morristown. "I was born in 1930 so it was already going on, but I know it was hard on everybody."

That was an understatement. Individuals all over the county were living in debt. A Volunteer Home Aid League was created in order to raise money and feed the masses during the holiday season in nearby Shelbyville. The Red Cross distributed numerous bags of flour from federal surplus supplies throughout the county, and school lunch programs were put in place in order to offer students nutritious meals.

"I don't think we ever realized what was going on," said Buchanan. "Everyone was in the same boat so it didn't occur to us that there were people who didn't have worn-out clothes."

By 1933, President Roosevelt had formed the Civil Works Administration and other federal programs to help people earn some form of wages. During this period, county commissioners took the opportunity to build a new courthouse and to replace the old "wagon" bridge over the Big Blue River. "Various other projects were also carried out in order to give employment to the needy," wrote McFadden. "A sewing group, which employed women to sew for the poor; several recreational programs with paid directors were instituted; adult education classes were conducted and a survey of county records were compiled."

For those living in Shelby County and dealing with their own set of problems, it was hard for them to believe that the problems of the Depression were widespread. Germany was under tremendous difficulty and willing to follow anyone who might lead the tattered nation back into a place of power. McFadden said that the people of Shelby County listened to the hysterical voice coming from the radio, and it wasn't long before Europe was once again at war and many of the continental countries were under Nazi control. As the draft was reinstituted in preparation for World War II, men were called into service, with many receiving their training at Camp Shelby in Mississippi, as well as at Camp Atterbury

"No one could get any nylons," remembered Virginia Williams. "There were a lot of things that suddenly you couldn't buy." The entire county was caught up in wartime activities, from bond rallies to blood drives and recyclable collections. Everywhere you looked, people were working for the war effort on the homefront. McFadden said that although the "fighting was far away its reality was much closer than it had been in 1918. In July 1942, the Council passed a black out ordinance setting penalties for the showing of lights when a black out was in effect."

The same month as the first blackout happened, Italian prisoners of war arrived at Camp Atterbury, and a subsequent camp was set up the following year in Morristown for German prisoners, who worked in the canning factory just down the street. Virginia Williams said it wasn't uncommon for people to go down and watch the novelty of the POWs at work. "I don't know why we did it," she said. "I guess we just wanted to see them."

Buchanan recalls the days when her mother worked in the canning factory and seeing the POWs throughout town. "We weren't afraid of them and mom got pretty close to a few of them. The prisoners dipped the tomatoes and brought them on trays to the peelers, which is what my mother's job was. I think she peeled more tomatoes than anyone."

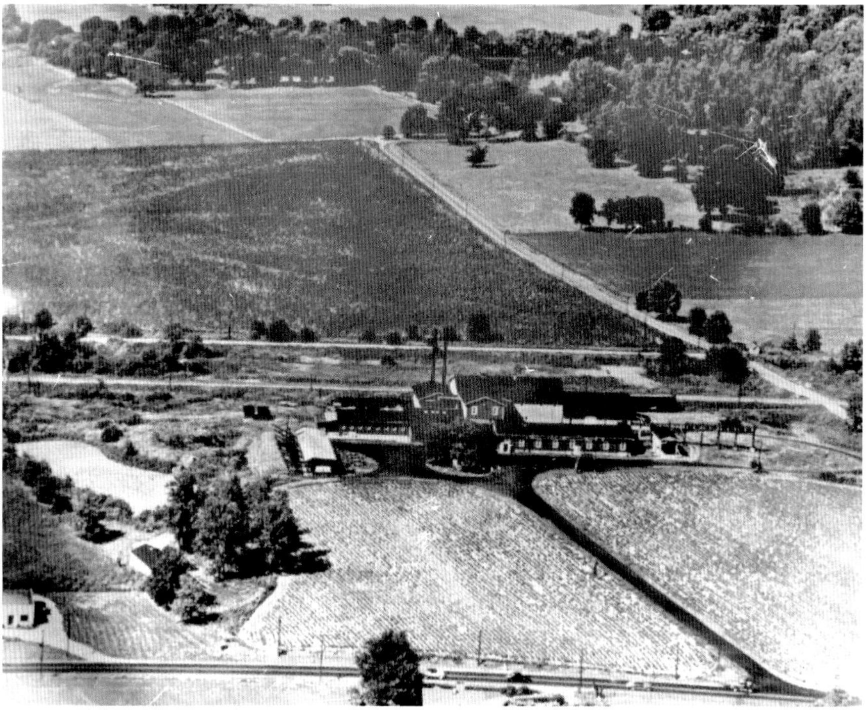

The Morristown Cannery was the place of employment for many German and Italian POWs during the war years. In peacetime, the cannery preserved pumpkin, tomatoes, corn and peas until better technology changed the way food was kept. *Courtesy of Donna Tracy at the Blue Bird Restaurant.*

Shelby County's history explains that the canning industry was one of the most important businesses to the county's economy. It began in the first decade of the twentieth century, and many additional canning factories began operations in the 1920s. Some of them failed during the Great Depression and most of them all but vanished in the 1960s with the advent of frozen foods and better technology for keeping fruits and vegetables preserved. For those who lived and worked around the canneries though, the factories provided incomes for families and were able to help provide various jobs during the war years.

"We used to go down to the cannery after school," said Buchanan. "Back then no one had a babysitter or after-school care so we would just walk down there and wait for our mothers, playing ball in the field right next to it or whatever. It was a different time back then and we didn't know any better."

A Soldier's Story

Though some of the men from Shelby County had to remain at home in order to help out on the family farm or their draft number wasn't high enough for them to be called for active duty, a number of men were quickly inducted and sent to Camp Atterbury and other locations for training.

Sherman Williams grew up in Morel Township during the Great Depression. He was a portrait of those who were defined as the "Greatest Generation." He inspired nearly everyone he met. He called the Depression the great equalizer when living in Morristown because "everybody was broke," and many were living with the assistance of the trustees. "My mother worked in the cannery as well as the Blue Bird Restaurant to make ends meet but everyone worked together to make the best of a bad situation. You could always tell the poor kids by the kind of shirt they wore. We all had the same shirt, but at least we were all equal," he said in an interview.

Williams described living in Morristown as a happy experience where everyone got along with everybody else, and after he graduated from the Morristown public school system, he became engaged, but he kept putting off the wedding date because he knew sooner or later he would end up going to war. "I was working at Borden's Dairy when I enlisted and soon headed off to Camp Atterbury," he said.

He also trained as a medic in Tennessee, where he learned how to care for wounds that soldiers would experience fighting on the front lines in the European Theater. In 1944, he was first sent to England, where he stayed until embarking for France in the second wave of the Normandy invasion. "I served at the Bulge and spent time in Holland, Belgium and Germany," he noted.

Once Europe was secured, Williams was trained with a weapon, and he assumed he would soon be headed to Japan. He said that he didn't use a weapon in Germany, and the Germans typically didn't fire on the medics, but he knew that wouldn't be the case in the Pacific. So when he heard that President Truman had ordered the bomb that ended the war dropped on Japan, Williams was relieved. "He added sixty years onto my life," he said with a laugh.

Williams saved some souvenirs that he brought back from the war, including a German youth knife, a dress dagger that was taken from a German officer at a stockade and several German medals, as well as his own commendations received for his service. In his later years, he received letters from President George W. Bush and the French government thanking him for his service.

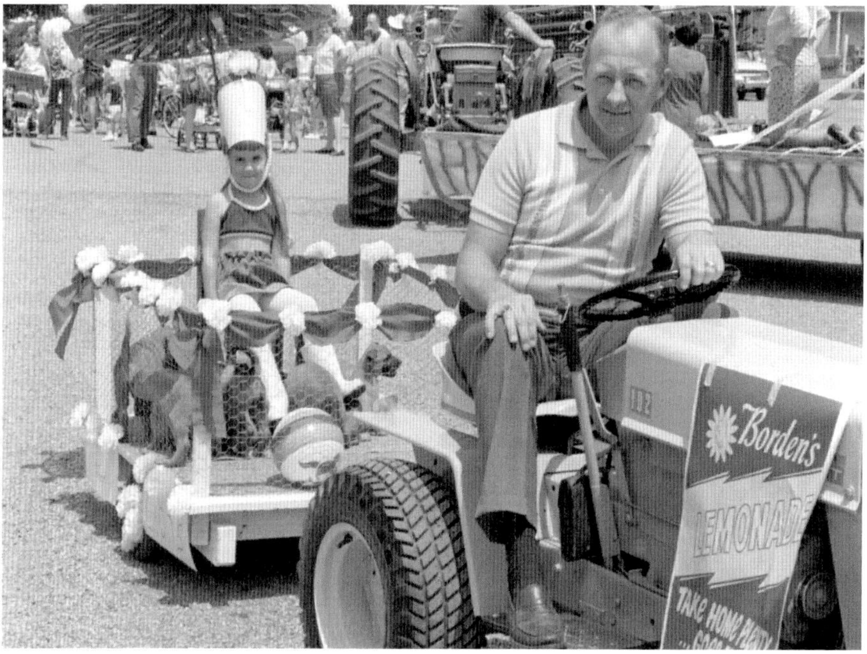

Sherman Williams pulls his niece Laura Buchanan during the Derby Days parade. Williams served in World War II at the Normandy invasion as well as in the Battle of the Bulge. *Courtesy of Donna Tracy at the Blue Bird Restaurant.*

After the war, Williams returned to Morristown. His engagement had ended while he was in Europe, but in 1950, he met the woman who would become his wife. He went back to work at the dairy, where he remained one of Elsie the Cow's best friends for forty-six years, working the condensing pan at plants in Morristown and Indianapolis.

After retiring in 1987, Williams lived a quiet life in Morristown, serving as a surrogate uncle, brother, father and friend to any number of locals. He hung out at the Blue Bird with his friends and was a lifetime member of the American Legion. Despite the hardships he had encountered, he felt that he lived in the greatest period of time, when no one had to lock their doors and everyone had time to visit. "Life is too fast now compared to the '30s and '40s," he said, noting that he had no regrets about his life, not even the war. "I wouldn't want to do it again, but I am glad that I was there."

Though victory was slow in coming, GIs returning to Morristown as well as other parts of the county were thrilled to be back on American soil. The end of the war signaled the end of the gas, sugar and meat rationing that had imposed hardships on the homefront. There was no longer a sense that peace would reign forever, as there had been at the end of the First World War, but rather a quiet awareness that any idea of peace and prosperity would be hard fought and a constant struggle to maintain. Morristown's American Legion remains an active part of the community, holding annual Memorial Day exercises in Asbury Cemetery and participating in the town's annual Derby Days.

Derby Days

No one knows what year the annual soapbox derby began, but it is a tradition that has been around for more than sixty years and helps define the community of 1,200. During the last weekend in July, U.S. 52 is blocked to traffic while the town holds a two-day celebration with parades, fish fries, community events and, of course, the big soapbox derby race down the large hill on the east end of town.

Jeff Decker, an *Indianapolis Star* correspondent, says that the scene around Morristown during Derby Days resembles a Norman Rockwell painting. "The Race was originally run on North Street, one block north of the current course…In the race's formative years boys raced their cars for distance. Today's derby pits two cars at a time against each other in a race to the bottom of the hill," he wrote.

Decker noted that the cars have changed, too, over the years. In the beginning, soapbox derby racers were entirely homemade, but now, more sophisticated designs are available, and some of the racers resemble rocket ships. Once the better racers were available, the more money mom and dad were putting into the car made competition fierce, despite the race being billed as a "family event."

Morristown's race is the great equalizer. All of the cars are alike, built by the Cub Scouts and leased to the parents for use in the race. The scouts give their cars a distinctive design with removable decals, and the race itself boils down to a straight run.

Over the years, the Derby Days festivities have grown, and recent years have seen fireworks, live music performances and even a midway to help the town celebrate. Derby Days serves as a homecoming for former residents of the community or graduates of Morristown High School. Race participants come from Morristown, Greenfield, Fountaintown and other nearby areas and love being part of the festivities. Buchanan said, "Everyone comes home

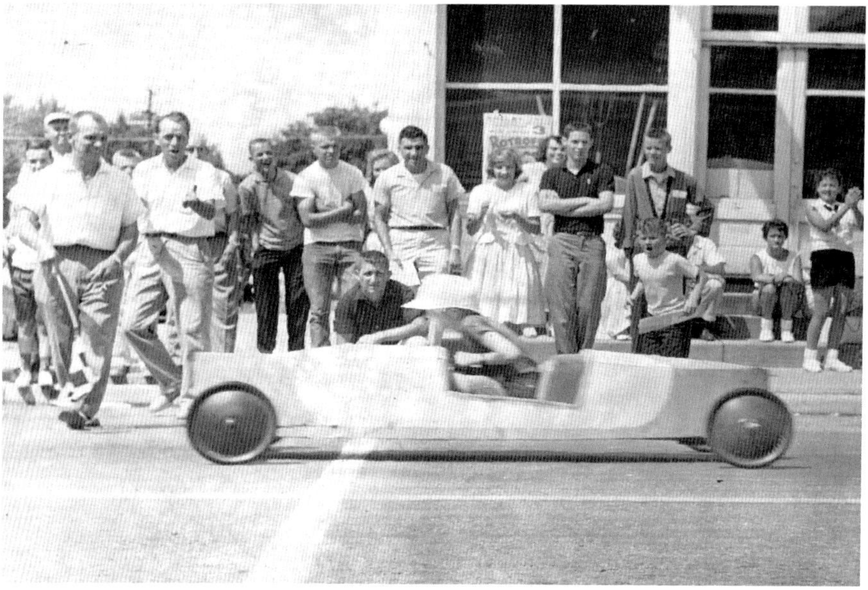

Scenes from the Morristown Derby Days. Scouts race to the bottom of the hill on U.S. 52 in hopes of being celebrated as the champion of the race. *Courtesy of Donna Tracy at the Blue Bird Restaurant.*

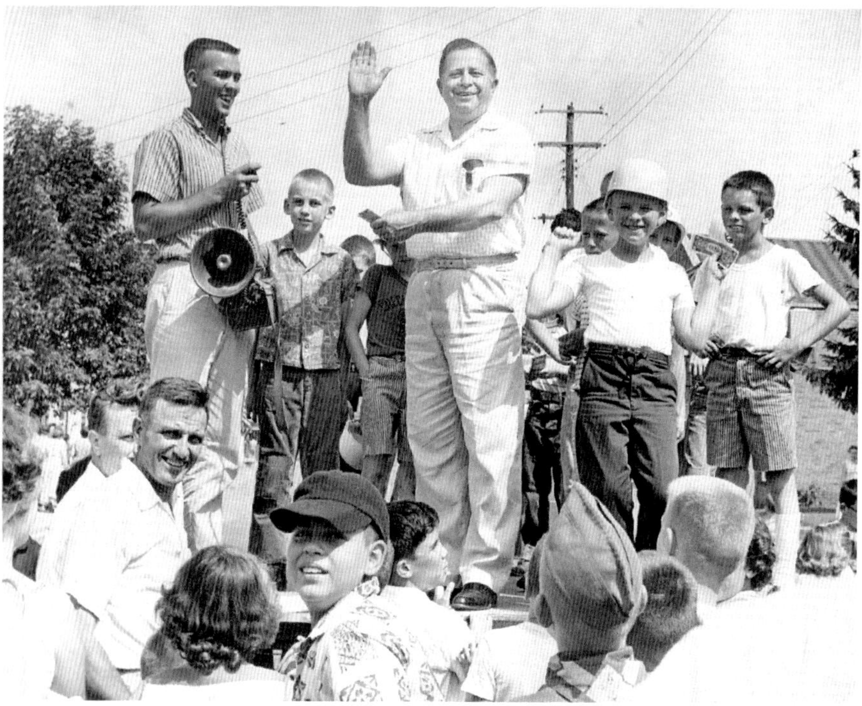

for the derby. People show up from a lot of the surrounding areas such as Indianapolis, New Palestine, and Greenfield in addition to towns all over Shelby County. The Derby is a big deal and it highlights Morristown as a great American community."

Derek Huff participated in several soapbox races during his tenure in the Morristown scouting movement. He said the experience not only taught him a lot about competition but also gave him practical experience working with power tools and getting the car prepared for the competition. "It's a lot of fun and I have had some really cool cars, including a Chevy Monte Carlo designed to look like Jeff Gordon's NASCAR," he said. "It's a great activity for kids."

Chapter 5

THE CAMP ATTERBURY CONNECTION

Located on the border of Shelby and Johnson Counties is Edinburgh, a town known as a shopping destination for its outlet mall and local amenities. Edinburgh was the first settlement in the Johnson County area and serves the greater Shelby County district as well. The first settler in the community was John Campbell, who moved to Edinburgh in 1820. The town was platted two years later, and lots were owned by Alexander Thompson and Lewis Bishop.

No one knows for certain how the town earned the name Edinburgh, but it is widely believed that the Scotch ancestry of Thompson played a major role in giving the town its name based on the capital city of Scotland. Others suggest that Edinburgh was so named because the early settlers saw Edinburgh as an "Eden" full of great beauty.

CAMP ATTERBURY

The entity that seems so linked to the Shelby County portion of Edinburgh is Camp Atterbury, which is today the training base for the Indiana National Guard. Planned months before the United States entered World War II, the site was recommended to Congress in 1941, and construction began the day after the attack on Pearl Harbor. About 1,500 frame buildings were designed and constructed to hold more than one army infantry division.

The camp also housed Wakeman General and Convalescent Hospital, a forty-seven-bed, two-story building that was one of the largest hospitals of its kind in the country for that era. The hospital was known for plastic eye replacements.

Some of the notable divisions that trained at Camp Atterbury during World War II included the 30th, 83rd, 92nd and 106th Infantry Divisions, and 39th Evacuation Hospital. The 106th left camp and was on the front lines within two weeks, serving in the Battle of the Bulge. Records show that seven thousand members of the division were reported missing in action (MIA), killed in action (KIA) or wounded in action (WIA).

After World War II, the base was essentially forgotten, but when the Korean War got underway, Camp Atterbury came alive once again, with the Twenty-eighth and Thirty-first Infantry Divisions stationed there. After 1954, the base was given to the Indiana National Guard to be used as a training base, and in the years following September 11, 2001, Camp Atterbury routinely trains activated regular and reserve forces prior to deployment to places such as Afghanistan and Iraq. It is the place where thousands of men and women say goodbye to their families as they leave in hopes of creating a better and safer country for the ones they love.

Camp Atterbury was initially a forty-three-thousand-acre site but has downsized to thirty thousand acres. The remainder of the original property is now utilized by the Atterbury Job Corps, the Indiana Department of Natural Resources (DNR), Hoosier Horse Park and the Johnson County Parks Department.

The Prisoner of War Camp

One of the most intriguing stories to come out of the Camp Atterbury legend is that of the prisoner of war camp that was maintained at the base during World War II. Originally, the POW camp encompassed forty-five acres and was designed to house three thousand prisoners of war. According to Cindy Morris, who wrote a paper on the POW camp when she was in eighth grade, Colonel Welton M. Modisette let folks in the area know that the POWs were available for laborious duties. He also vowed to treat the prisoners humanely and with a sympathetic dignity.

The first shipment of POWs arrived on April 30, 1943. They were Italians who had been captured during the North Africa Campaign and then brought to Camp Atterbury. Those who were sick or wounded were sent to the post hospital, and Morris noted that there was a high level of colic, sand malaria and other ailments among the POWs.

"Processing began the next day so the prisoners would have time to rest after their long journey," Morris wrote. "Each prisoner had an interview concerning his name, age, rank in the army, army occupation, civilian occupation, serial number, and name and address of his nearest living relative."

The prisoners were expected to adhere to the same discipline as any other member of the military. English classes were conducted, in which prisoners learned the national anthem. They were also instructed about the basic military courtesies so that they would be able to recognize rank and insignia. Prisoners were required to send a card to their family members letting them know that they were safe and being treated well, and they were issued a barracks bag, a hat, two coats, two blankets, a toiletry set, a razor, two pairs of shoes, a belt, two pairs of pants, two sets of underwear, four pairs of socks and two shirts.

Those in the camp said that discipline was not harsh and the rules were clear. Prisoners were not allowed to have weapons, women or pets, and they were permitted to move about freely within the compound. They were even allowed to receive visitors. Morris said that the German prisoners who found themselves at Camp Atterbury were given special treatment.

> *According to the rules of the Geneva Convention, the American Army had to get orderlies for the German officers. These orderlies were German enlisted men. A German officer could not be made to work outside the compound or on civilian projects. They specifically requested remunerative occupations, and could not be assigned to supervisory work unless it could not be done by another prisoner. These German officers were paid their allowances according to their rank in the army. For warrant officers and first and second lieutenants, their allowance was the equivalent of $20 a month, for captains, it was $30 a month and for anyone with the rank of major or above, it was $40. These officers were reluctant to work at first, but after seeing the other men earning money, they soon changed their minds.*

Peter Von Seildein of Stuttgart, Germany, was a POW at the camp after being wounded in Normandy and taken prisoner on August 20, 1944. He described life at Camp Atterbury as "heaven," a place where prisoners were given standard clothing, plenty to eat and a bed to sleep in.

> *For the first few months, I was working in one of the 12 kitchens within the POW camp, but I found this rather tiresome and volunteered for work*

> *outside the camp. There is hardly a menial job I didn't do the next year; picking tomatoes and apples, working in a slaughterhouse, driving a tractor, pressing shirts and trousers, washing dishes, and so on…During the winter I was an orderly in an officers' club in Camp Atterbury, cleaning up the club and serving on the bar. My last POW job was interpreting for an "ash and trash" detail, which had to clean up barracks after they were left by discharged soldiers—one of the most sought after jobs as the GIs left all and everything behind that they couldn't carry with them in the barracks.*

Von Seildein was at Camp Atterbury for nearly twenty-two months before being sent to France, where he worked in another POW camp until his discharge on July 20, 1946.

Other prisoners counted on their spirituality to get them through their time at the POW camp. One of the lasting and endearing aspects of the POW era was the construction of the POW chapel, known as the Chapel in the Meadow. The prisoners received permission to construct the chapel in 1943 using surplus materials from the other projects at the camp. After World War II, the chapel fell into disrepair, but it was restored in the late 1980s and rededicated on September 16, 1989. Recently, a twentieth-anniversary commemorative event was held to celebrate the rededication of the chapel. David Pagnucco attended the ceremony. His father, Fioravante Luigi Pagnucco, had been a POW at the camp and was one of the men who had helped build the chapel more than sixty-five years before.

"I am interested in Italian culture, what my father went through at Camp Atterbury and to see where he was stationed," he said in an interview with the *Criterion* Catholic newspaper.

Pagnucco's father was a man of tremendous faith, like many of the Italian POWs detained at the camp. It was this faith that led them to build the chapel, which consists of a small altar, a statue of the Virgin Mary and two cherubs that seem to be crowning the Blessed Mother. It is rumored that the prisoners even used their own blood to obtain the red hue they needed in the original painting.

Monsignor Joseph F. Schaedel, the vicar general for the Archdiocese of Indianapolis, celebrated Mass at the chapel and praised the men whose faith in God helped them keep going even though they were far from home. "Where did they get the strength to continue to believe?" Schaedel asked in his homily at the commemorative Mass. "They got it from the 'living bread that came from heaven' given to them by their priest chaplain."

Chapter 6

FAIRLAND AND BOGGSTOWN

When Isaac Odell first spotted the stretch of land fifteen minutes southeast of Indianapolis, he declared it a "fair land on which to build a town." His friend Henry Jenkins agreed, and the two of them founded Fairland in 1852.

Fairland is a small town with many big-city conveniences. Its past is richly steeped in a Christian tradition, as noted by the number of early churches

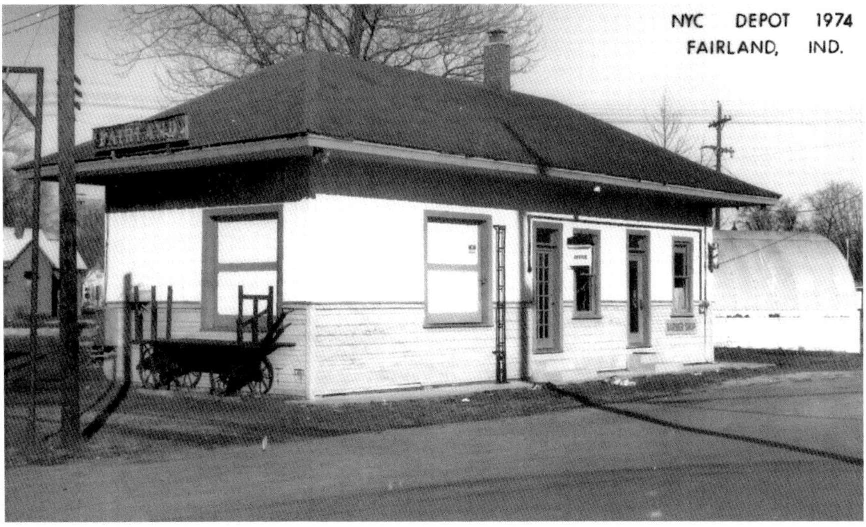

Fairland Station shows the importance of train travel throughout Shelby County. From transport to Indianapolis and Cincinnati, the railroads were the cash cows of the community.

that were founded within the community. In fact, the Woman's Society of Christian Service, a ministry of the Fairland Methodist Church, chronicles some of those early congregations in its *Hoosier Recipes from Fairland Kitchens* cookbook, published in 1952.

FAIRLAND CHURCHES

Other than a mercantile operated by Isaac Tull in 1854, the landscape was predominately made up of homes and congregations. Fairland Methodist Church was the first church community to be established in Fairland. According to the cookbook, the church was part of the Sugar Creek Circuit, which was composed of two hundred members and two church buildings. Reverend A.F. Schafer was appointed for the first year, and in the following eight years, a different pastor served each subsequent year.

"In 1855, the name of the charge was changed from Sugar Creek to London charge and Rev. Matthew Mitchell was appointed as pastor. The following year, Rev. W. Winchester was the pastor and a new church edifice was commenced at Fairland," reads the cookbook. The building was completed and dedicated three years later.

"Such was the strength of the people that the circuit's name changed from Sugar Creek to Fairland, and preachers were heard in places such as Fairland, Boggstown, Center, Brandywine, and Ellis Schoolhouse," reports the book.

As the community grew, there were a number of clergy members who ministered to the people of Fairland, living in the parsonage that was constructed for their use. In 1878, a League of One Hundred Ladies was formed, and this group was influential in its ability to procure funds for the needs of the church. At this time, the membership continued to grow, and the Fairland Methodist Church boasted three hundred congregants.

Eventually, the original Methodist church building was sold to Adolph Richtner, who moved the entire building to Main Street with designs to use the structure as an opera house. According to the published history, many productions were presented in the former church building, from traveling troupes to local talent.

The new church was dedicated in 1900, and the new parsonage was completed four years later. In 1925, work began on the new basement. The total cost for the project was about $6,000, but the diligence of the community and faithful cooperation brought this project to a speedy conclusion.

Despite the Great Depression raging around them, an exciting thing was happening at the Methodist church in 1935. A radio program was held for twelve Sunday mornings with fourteen other churches participating in the event. "The programs were 30 minutes in length and went out over WFBM by remote control," reads the history. "D.G. Gordon was the manager and announcer and Hubert Marshall was the director of music."

It was an exciting time as the postwar years continued to bring modern changes and conveniences to the congregation. Today, the Fairland United Methodist Church and the New Life United Methodist Church remain important components in the community, and the United Methodist Women's group, just like its predecessor, the League of One Hundred Ladies, continues to accomplish a lot for local and global missions, helping women and children everywhere.

The Fairland Baptist Church began in Brandywine on July 30, 1832. According to a published source, the land for the original building was donated by Levy Morgan and was along Brandywine Creek and the old Michigan Road. Without a formal minister, the services were presided over each week, in turn, by an elder of the church. "Business meetings were held on the first Saturday of each month at the home of the various members," reads the brief history in the local cookbook.

In March 1859, it was decided to move the church to Fairland, and the congregation purchased property from Daniel Bradley. The construction was completed in 1860, with Reverend J. Reece officiating. The following year, the Sunday school was established, and in 1904 the women of the congregation organized the Ladies' Aid Society.

The Baptist movement remains strong in the Fairland community, and there are still several Baptist churches in the area making their mark and doing plenty of good works for their congregations and people elsewhere, spreading the word of God and bringing people to Christ.

According to the legend, the Church of Christ worshipping in Fairland was organized under the auspices of the Indiana Christian Organization by Walter S. Smith. Smith was an evangelist and was assisted by his brother, who worked out of the First Christian Church in Chicago. "These two ministers came in and began work on October 28, 1890 in the old brick school building, which had been supplied with temporary seats and furnished with a stove and a half-dozen coal oil lamps. A pulpit was improvised from a dry goods box, and John K. Smith furnished an organ," reads the book.

Other handmade implements were used as well, and the evangelist brought with him his own supply of hymnals. As the church got underway, the charter members affixed their names to agree that they would "become members of an organization to be called The Church of Christ located for worship in this village, adopting for our government the New Testament, and agreeing to abide by its instructions in matter of faith and practice."

The Fairland Christian Church remains an integral part of the community. According to the church's website, the Fairland Christian Church is a community of "everyday people serving God by continuing the work Jesus Christ came to accomplish: 'For the Son of Man has come to seek and to save that which was lost' (Luke 19:10). We honor His love for us by believing in His death, burial, and resurrection; obeying His commands; and spreading His Gospel."

Town Development

Isaac Odell served as a draft officer during the Civil War, and several members of Company F were raised in the vicinity of Fairland. Odell was also responsible for platting additions to the town before being elected to represent the county in the 1869 state legislative session. He also made his way into the banking business and established Fairland Private Banking House. He studied law and was a justice of the peace. In fact, he died while giving a speech.

In 1873, the Sugar Creek Lodge No. 279, F&AM came to Fairland. The lodge began in 1861 when James Barngrover and others met in a Boggstown hall in order to organize a Masonic lodge. The charter was issued in 1862 under the most worshipful grand master John B. Fravel. Though the group met in Boggstown for three years, the members voted to move to Fairland in 1865.

It took another eight years for a building to be erected in the new location. Once it was, though, members met in the hall above what was commonly known as the R.T. Smith Store. In 1934, the Masons bought the building a few doors down from them that had previously been owned by the local Knights of Pythias chapter. This hall, too, was over a business establishment. For over a century, this venerated lodge has been hailed as a major part of the community.

The latter part of the 1800s offered the people of Fairland many other businesses and town amenities. Early businessmen included Harry Freeman, who was the editor of the *Fairland Bulletin*, a weekly newspaper; G.S. Harrell,

"HOOSIER RECIPES"

FROM

FAIRLAND KITCHENS

Sponsored

by

Woman's Society of Christian Service

of the

FAIRLAND METHODIST CHURCH

Fairland, Indiana

1952

The Fairland recipe book was published by the Women's Society at the Fairland Methodist Church. Not only was the book full of recipes, but it contained community history as well. *Courtesy of Virginia Williams.*

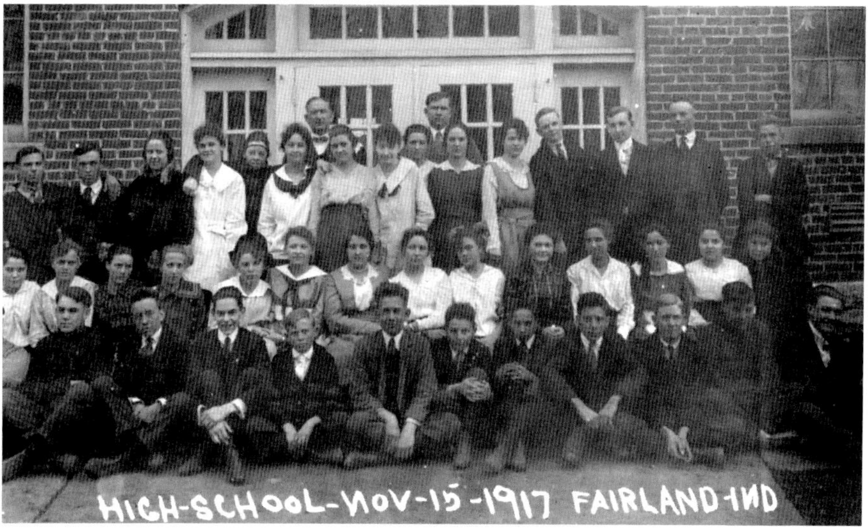

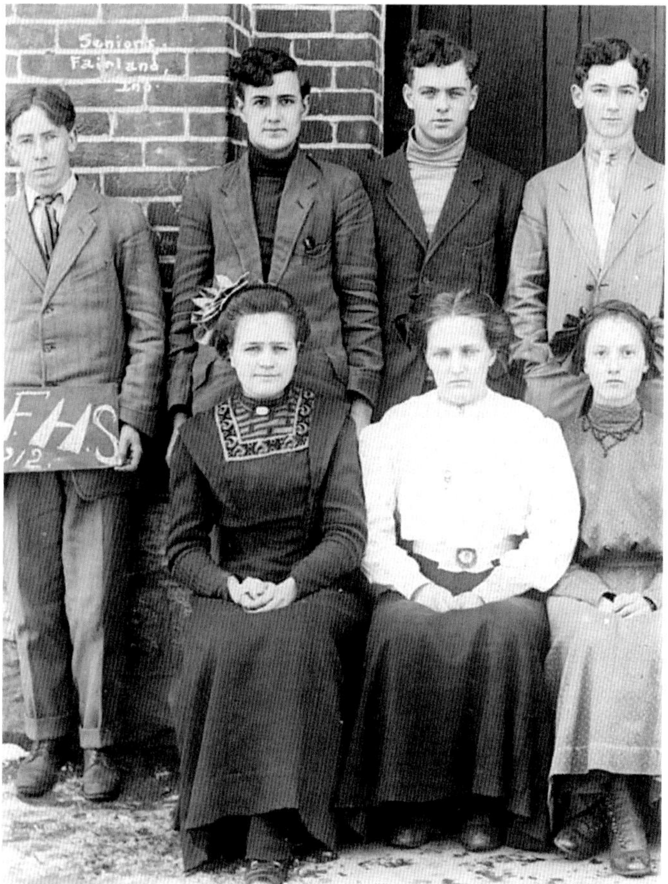

Above: A vintage picture of the Fairland High School graduating class of 1917. Eventually, three of the high schools in the area merged, and Triton Central was created.

Left: Another vintage picture of a Fairland High School class. The old Fairland High School building has been demolished and is now a park.

the proprietor of the hotel; and James McGollum, a blacksmith and wagon maker. Other members of the community opened shops, booteries, grocery stores and a doctor's office. Businessmen also included sawmill operators, grain dealers and a local postal delivery person.

Boggstown

According to a local website, Boggstown was platted in 1867 and named for Joseph Boggs, a man who ran the tobacco factory that made plug tobacco, which was sold via wagon throughout central Indiana and other parts of the Midwest. The community was eight miles northwest of Shelbyville and contained twenty-four lots. The earliest entities in the community included a general store, a post office and a blacksmith shop, in addition to the tobacco industry.

The small community's claim to fame occurred in 1861, when the town founders decided that in the event of a civil war, they would secede from the Union. For the most part, the resolution was merely talk, but

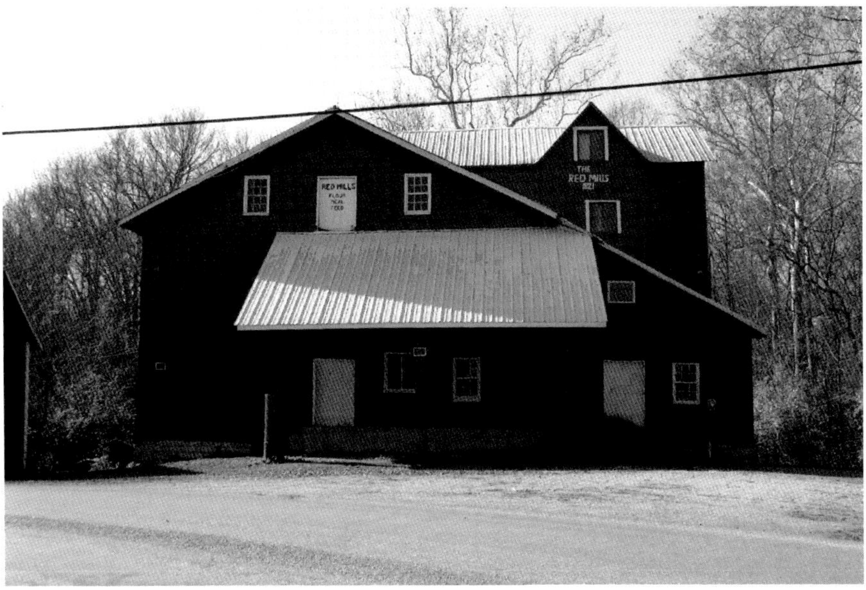

The Red Mills in Boggstown is an old building dating back to 1821. John Riley, a teacher at Scecina Memorial High School, remembers camping near the area with his family when he was a child. *Author's private collection.*

when war broke out, the resolution resurfaced and created a stir that gained the community notoriety throughout the southern and western regions of the country.

Today, Boggstown is famous for the Boggstown Cabaret, located in the historic Red Man's Lodge, which was built in 1873. According to the theatre's website, the building is situated overlooking the Cincinnati and Martinsville Railroad and is believed to be haunted. In 1884, the Boggstown Inn and Cabaret opened its doors and became a place that celebrated the art of piano and banjo music, which was popular during the turn of the last century and throughout the 1920s. With new ownership in 1999, the cabaret moved into the next century as a dinner theatre and live music venue that celebrates everything from Vegas to Branson.

"We used to have a family who had a lot of land down in Boggstown," said John Riley, a teacher at Scecina Memorial High School in Indianapolis. "I remember we used to go down there and pitch a tent and camp on the land. I never knew what if it was a farm or what. We just used to have a good time down there though."

TRITON CENTRAL HIGH SCHOOL

Though much has been discussed about the early educational opportunities for Shelby County children, Orville Branson Jr. wrote an article that outlines the original high schools and their consolidation into what is known today as Triton Central.

Fairland had its first graduating class in 1926, brandishing the colors of red and white, while nearby Boggstown High School opted for the menacing black and orange when it opened in 1924. Boggstown sported spirit colors of blue and gold. In 1958, the schools merged to become Triton Central High School, a school that was composed of three rich histories.

Branson wrote:

> *In the fall of 1962, the doors of the new Triton Central High opened. The trustees of the three townships served as the school board. A man by the name of Heller was supervising principal for the consolidation. The school district was under the county superintendent, Mr. Thomas Fogarty. Boggstown became Triton West Elementary and for the first two or three years, grades one through seven attended there. Moral Township became*

> *Triton North, and the Fairland building housed the eighth grade and high school. Rather odd arrangements due to space availability. When the new school was done, the High School (grades 9 to 12) moved into the new Triton Central High School building, and the Fairland School became the Junior High School. Sometime in the early 1970's, the new Elementary was built for grades K-6.*

Boggstown and Morel were closed prior to 1976, and ten years later, the new middle school was opened accommodating grades five through eight. Both the Boggstown and Fairland buildings have been demolished, and both areas are now parks.

Chapter 7

UNINCORPORATED COMMUNITIES

Throughout Shelby County, there are a number of small communities that help make up the fabric of this rich area of central Indiana. While some of them are merely memories, others are vibrant little bergs that residents are proud to call home and that have rich histories that add to the flavor of the townships in the region.

London

Located in Moral Township, London was platted in 1852 by Aaron House and composed of thirty-two lots. The town took off; a year later, there were fifty-five lots in the community. The town was anchored by the London Methodist Church, which was established in 1853 when a lot was purchased from Aaron and Margaret House for twenty-five dollars.

According to *The History of London and Brookfield Shelby County, Indiana*, the original church building served the community until about 1890, when it was remodeled to remove the balcony. A few years later in 1898, the church was destroyed by a fire, and a new church was constructed not long afterward under the ministry of Reverend J.P. Mason. While waiting for the new building, services were held in the school.

The exact date of the construction of the London School is unknown, but what is known is that in 1865 the lot on which it stood was sold by House.

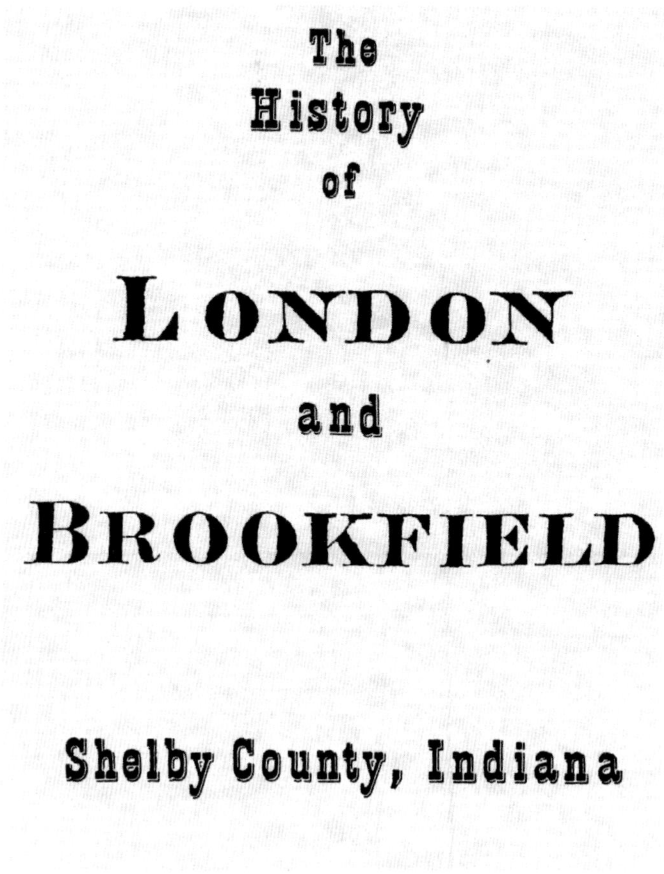
The History of LONDON and BROOKFIELD Shelby County, Indiana

The cover of the published history of London and Brookfield, highlighting early businesses and families of the area as well as clever anecdotes of local news. *Courtesy of Virginia Williams.*

Mamie Brandt recalled that the building she remembers in 1875 is not the same building that was there in later years. There were many teachers at the London School, including Volney Larson, Helen Guinn, Edwin Pritchard, Willard Means, Nannie Jordon and Amie Sutherland.

Those teachers took pride in the little schoolhouse, which was originally a frame structure before it was replaced by brick. The schoolhouse was eventually moved, and the lot was purchased by O.L. Means, who added a storeroom and used the building as a home where the telephone exchange was located. Bertha Walker is also known to have owned the building during the Great Depression with her son Tom, who was serving as the postmaster for the community. The first mail carrier for London was George B. "Bent" Jordon, a former schoolteacher who held the postal position for twenty-six years.

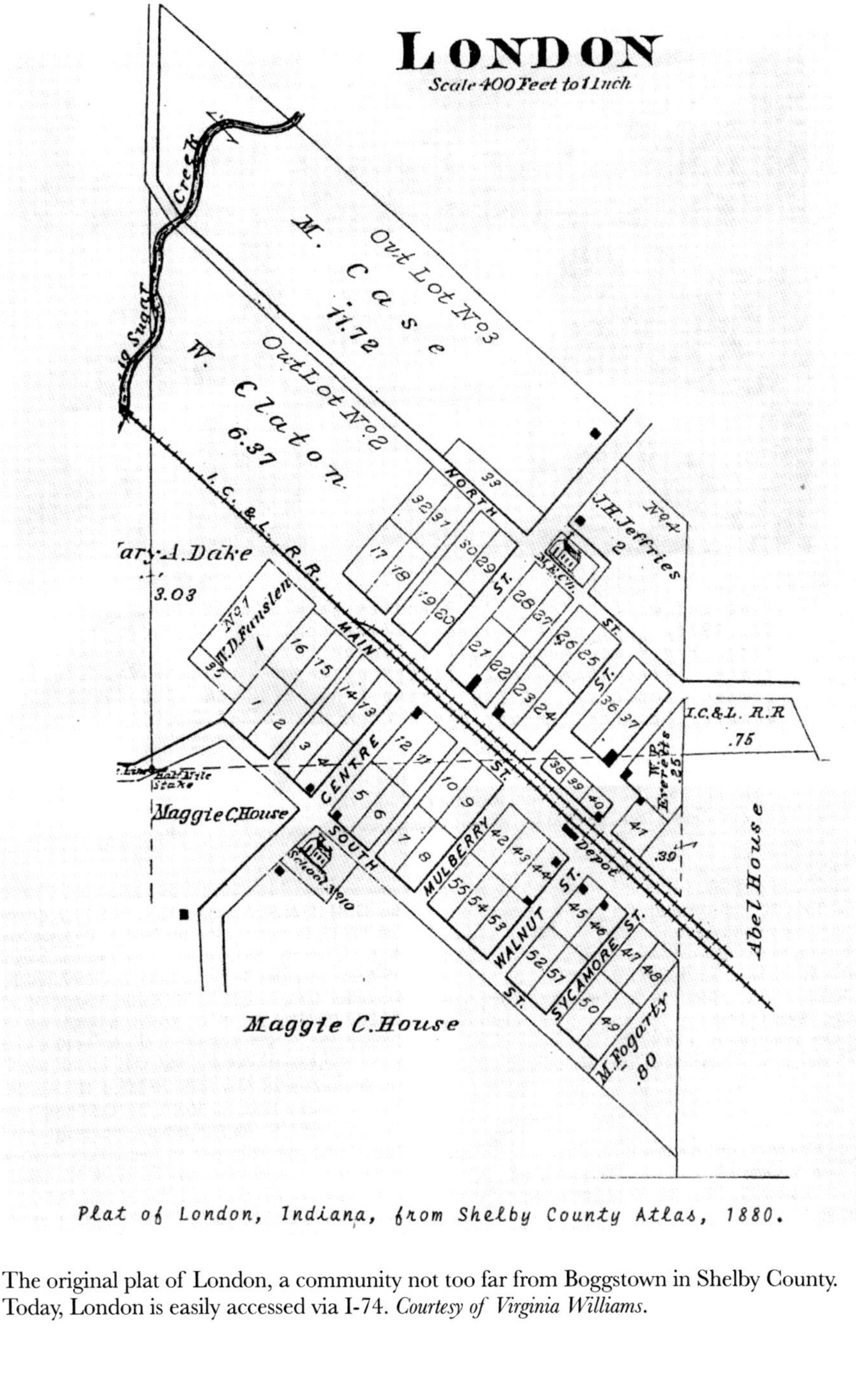

Plat of London, Indiana, from Shelby County Atlas, 1880.

The original plat of London, a community not too far from Boggstown in Shelby County. Today, London is easily accessed via I-74. *Courtesy of Virginia Williams.*

The last school building was one story and contained four rooms, two cloak rooms, a coal stove and no modern conveniences. According to the published history, students had to pump water from the well, which was the best in town, so it was used by everyone—with everyone using the same tin cup. There were two outside toilets accommodating all eight grades and the first two grades of high school. Commencements were held at the London Methodist Church. In 1912, the commencement notice had an admonition printed inside to warn everyone of the solemnity of the occasion:

> *All persons are warned against whispering, talking, or making any kind of disturbance whatever during the speaking. You are at liberty to talk and laugh during the music, but anyone disturbing the speaker will positively be arrested and the sheriff or his deputy is here for that purpose. Ladies will kindly remove their hats. Order of the County Board of Education, William Everson, Superintendent.*

One of the more prominent residents in London was Thomas Fogarty. He was born on November 11, 1889, and graduated from the London School. He went on to graduate from the Central Normal College in 1919 and earned his bachelor of arts degree from Franklin College and a master's degree from Indiana University. He began his teaching career in a one-room schoolhouse in Greenbay during the 1909–10 school year and went on to become the principal of the London School, as well as a coach. Throughout his career, Fogarty also served in Boggstown, Flat Rock and Waldron.

After marrying Matilda Vories and having one daughter, Virginia, Fogarty became the superintendent of the Shelby County school system in 1929 and held that post through 1965, never missing a day of work. Although the schools were consolidated and reduced in number, his fifty-four-year career is not insignificant. He was also the superintendent of the Southwest district from 1957 to 1959. A proud veteran of World War I and a Mason, his memberships included Phi Delta Kappa, the American Legion, Veterans of Foreign Wars, the Century Club and the State Teacher's Association. Upon his death, he was buried at Forest Hill Cemetery, but London has not forgotten his contribution to the community or the county.

One of the earliest physicians in London was Dr. Oral Holmes McDonald. A graduate of Indiana Medical College, Dr. McDonald began his practice in London in 1904, marrying his wife, Emma, two years later. "Dr. McDonald was a good physician, sometimes did dental work and was a taxidermist," reads the entry on the doctor in the published history of London. "He was interested in his community, organized an Audubon Bird Society and rented a house in London for a boys' club."

The boys spent time at the club playing croquet, poker and loafing around. The house was heated with coal, which the boys found along the railroad track, dropped by the cars. The doctor himself lived in a brick home, which was eventually moved to the location of his farm just east of Little Broadripple on 500 North. Though he moved his family to Kentucky, where he became the administrator of the veterans' hospital, like many who left, he returned to Indiana with his wife, and they lived the remainder of their lives on their farm until Emma died in 1954. The doctor followed her a year later. They are both buried at Boggstown Cemetery.

When it came to businesses in London, grocery stores were certainly a popular area of commerce. David Tucker was the owner of a general store on lot 12 in London. It was a two-story building that was originally built in 1856 as a seminary. The post office was in the building as well, but Tucker also had a traveling wagon that made the rounds carrying goods and staples to those who couldn't make the trip into town. A potbellied stove sat in the back room, where men came and passed the time. Ladies and children of course gathered in the front of the store, where kids helped themselves

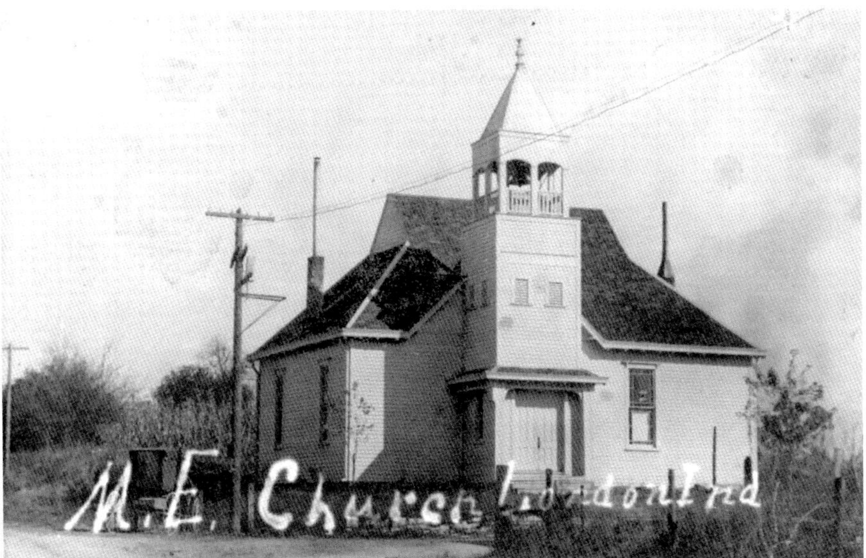

A vintage postcard of London's Methodist Episcopal Church. Though there is no date, from the wagon in the photo, it looks to be from the late 1800s.

to barrels of peanuts and played with the soap on the shelves. When their extremities finally came to rest, many of the kids fell asleep in the store.

After Tucker left the store, the back room was used for "traveling medicine shows," and popcorn was served as a popular refreshment during the entertainment. During the 1930s, Roscoe and Edna Crum operated the store. The couple used part of the space as a dance hall with live entertainment where local square dancers would perform. The venue was very popular with the locals, but about 1940, the building was razed.

Oliver Means had a grocery store as well as grain interests in Brookfield, Acton and Fairland. He was the postmaster from 1889 to 1893, followed by his wife, Ella, who held the job until 1897. He had the post again before he gave it up in 1905. The couple eventually moved to Shelbyville and opened a department store. Eventually, Willard Means sold the store to Harry Harrell, but the facility went through several owners between 1893 and 1962.

Of course, London had its access to interurban and railroad transportation. The Big Four ran on the south-side railroad tracks, while the interurban ran on the north-side. Farmers used the interurban to haul milk cans. Everett Fritts recalled riding in the seat of a wagon with his father and grandfather, Clarence and Rueben Fritts, as they drove hogs to London to be shipped by rail to the Indianapolis stockyards. For the published history of London, he said that the loading pens for cattle and hogs were near the interurban and railroad tracks. The coal yard was located in the same area.

London had its own saloon near the railroad and interurban lines, which was a popular place. It even featured its own bull pen for those who became intoxicated and unruly and had to spend the night. The high fence surrounding it discouraged any breakouts.

Another form of transportation for London was the jitney. While most people think of the jitney as the bus that takes New Yorkers to the Hamptons for the weekend, the London jitney was the rental service available in lieu of a livery stable. "In the summer Billy Coons and Dan Smith met the early interurban cars and took fishermen on Saturday and Sunday to certain spots along Big Sugar and Buck Creek," reads the published history of London. "They each had a surrey and an old plug horse. They picked up their passengers at a designated time to return to the interurban station."

Among the other entities in London was the grain elevator that burned to the ground in 1936 and was never rebuilt. The sawmill and lumberyard, purchased by William "Bill" Fogarty for $700, was another major employer in the community. Some of the workers worked inside the mill while others worked in the field cutting trees and hauling logs. One of the biggest stories to come out of the mill was the death of Jesse Means, who died when he was cutting a tree. The mill eventually burned down in the 1920s and ceased operations in 1937.

The telephone was a major modern convenience enjoyed by some homeowners in London, and over the years, the exchange or switchboard was operated in a variety of locations around town. Usually, a home served as the best place for the hub. During those years, operators included Joe Crum, Frank Weaver, Rolla Means and Amelia Mease.

For a period of time about 1912, the exchange was located in the back of the grocery store when Mease was the operator, but she gave it up when she became sick a few years later. The exchange was taken over by Mabel Smith in 1916. Eventually, however, the phone company bought the Willard Means residence in order to keep the exchange in one location. Mabel and Carolyn Smith were operators until 1934.

The exchange moved again and was located behind another grocery store during the time Marshall and Alice King owned it. In 1942, it switched hands again and was operated by Sam and Virginia Neel. Several other people ran the exchange until it was sold to the Indiana Bell System in the late 1940s.

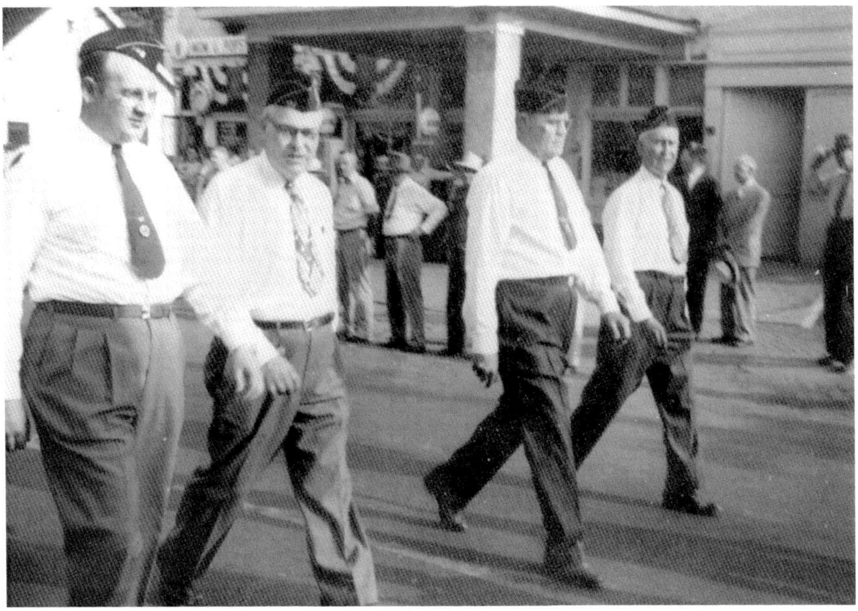

Groups such as the American Legion, the Masons, the Odd Fellows and other service organizations have always made Shelby County a strong community. *Courtesy of Donna Tracy at the Blue Bird Restaurant.*

London also had plenty of fraternal organizations. These groups performed a number of service projects for the community and inspired a lot of community pride. One of the largest was the Oskaloosa Tribe of Red Men's Lodge (a name that would no doubt spark some controversy today), which organized a parade to the cemetery for the town's Memorial Day celebration. London also had active Knights of Pythias and Ku Klux Klan chapters.

Brookfield

Brookfield is located in the southwest part of Moral Township near the Johnson County–Marion County line. Robert Means and Joshua Dearmin platted the town in November 1863. There were thirty-two lots established, with sixteen of them located on the north side of the railroad tracks and the remainder of them on the south side.

The town was originally a trading post until the railroad was completed. Early settlers in the community included John Joyce, a pioneer merchant who had his business until 1860, when E.H. Stanley took it over. Stanley had a history of being in the mercantile and grain business, but during the Civil War he also served as a postmaster.

Fountain Means was another early citizen who operated a general store for a few years. He sold the business to W.C. Means. According to the *History of London and Brookfield*, "Cornelius Means was also in the merchandising business at Brookfield in 1860. After enlisting and serving in Co. F, 47th Regiment Infantry, he returned to Brookfield in 1867, beginning the mercantile business as the partner of his brother, Caleb F. Means. This business union lasted 16 years."

The Means brothers bought the store from John K. Smith and were able to create a large trade by being fair with their customers, having a large stock and keeping their profit margins small. Accounts show that they were very successful, more so than other merchants in the area. Their success even meant that they had a half share in the gristmill. Cornelius was a man of many talents, serving not only as the postmaster but also as a ticket agent for the Big Four Railroad and as a notary. In 1882, he sold his interest in the store to J.J. Stanley, and after he came onboard, the firm of Mean and Stanley was the leading retail establishment in town.

In 1869, the grain house was converted into a gristmill, and Stanley served as half owner. Frank Mann operated the livery stable. Business was

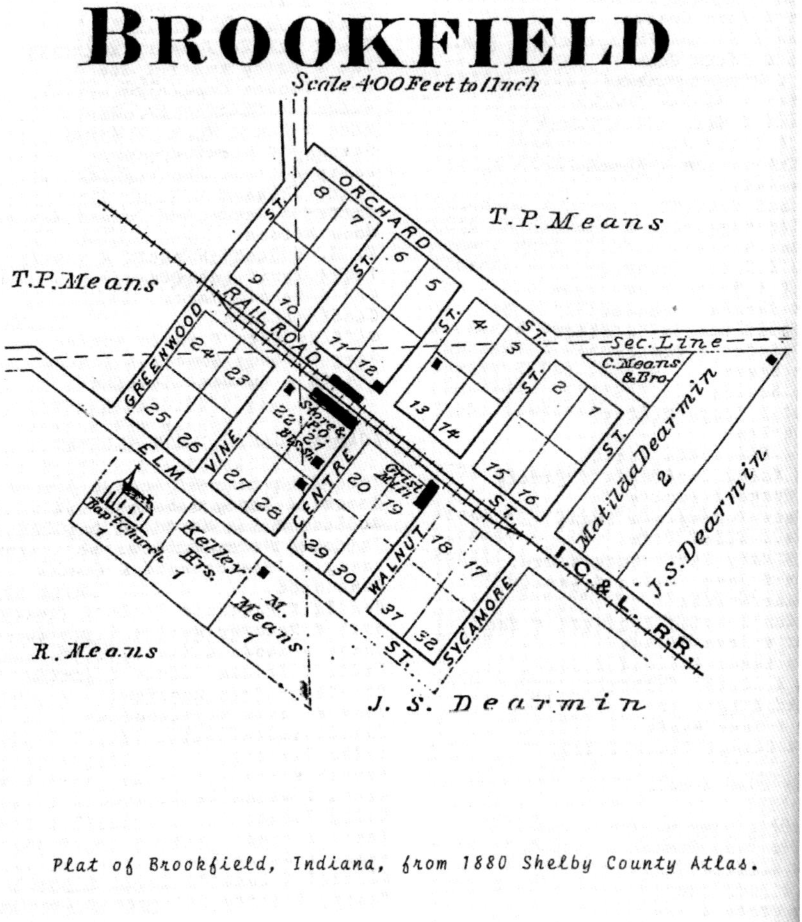

The original plat of Brookfield in 1863 contained thirty-two lots. The community was designed by Robert Means and Joshua Dearmin. *Courtesy of Virginia Williams.*

booming in Brookfield, and Thomas Smock purchased a blacksmith shop in the community in 1890. He had lots of experience, having operated one in Pleasant View for thirty-six years. The one in Brookfield was equally successful, and he ran it until 1904, when Means took it over. In addition, there was a sawmill located across the street from the school, the gristmill and the general store. Brookfield's post office succeeded Pleasant View, with early postmasters including Warren Steacy, William Means and Henderson Stanley.

Brookfield had phone lines before the Bell Company entered the area. Various women operated the switchboard, which was hooked up to the London network. At the time, phone service wasn't a twenty-four-hour operation, and families had to contend with a party line system. If there was an emergency, subscribers were out of luck if the operator was asleep.

The People

Brookfield and London have been home to many well-established names synonymous with the community. Frank Andrews was among them. Andrews was a local farmer who was born in 1882. During his lifetime, he was very active in the community as a member of the Masons in Fairland and the Knights of Pythias in London. He played on a local baseball team and was married to Bessie Waggoner, who was the daughter of Catherine Conner Waggoner, a relative of the Conners of Conner Prairie fame. The couple settled on a farm just east of London on North 700, where they had one daughter named Alberta, born in 1908. Andrews died of exertion after chasing dogs away from his sheep.

As for Bessie, she remained active until her death, working as an employee at the State Income Tax Division. She was a past deputy of the Eastern Star (Fairland Chapter) and a member of the White Shrine, Pythian Sisters, Shelby County Garden Club, Women's Study Club and the London Methodist Church. The couple is buried in the New Palestine Cemetery.

Joel Crum hailed from Dauphin County, Pennsylvania, and moved to Indiana by way of Cincinnati and on through Madison, where he planned to continue northward to Indianapolis. He made it as far as Sugar Creek, where he found the land to his liking. He went back to Pennsylvania long enough to marry his wife, Maria Jeffries, in 1839, and then moved his new bride and her parents to Sugar Creek, where Crum farmed the land, while his brothers-in-law worked as carpenters. Though he was known as a businessman and a farmer, Crum sold off all of his business interests in order to build another farm one and a half miles east of London. When the Civil War broke out, his oldest son enlisted, slowing the work on the homes that Crum was building on the land. Eventually, a new hand was trained to do the work, and the home became the site of many weddings and the birthplace for the younger children of the family.

Crum was considered to be one of the more well-to-do farmers of his day, and he was known for being an honest Christian man who was very generous with his family. He died on August 1, 1893, and is buried in the Crum mausoleum in London Cemetery.

Flat Rock

The original settlement in the Flat Rock area was established about two and a half miles from its present location. It was named after the Flat Rock River, which is a literal translation of the original Indian name of *Pack-op-ka* or *Puchachism.* Initially, the settlement was located on the south side of the river, and it was about 1823 when Isaac Drake established a mill on the land. Drake also served as the first postmaster in the area, and no doubt, the "post office" was located in the mill.

The first frame church was built just east of the mill. Some of its early members included Thomas Wooley, Richard Drake, Peter Messick and Zachariah Vansycle. The popularity of the Flat Rock area made it an

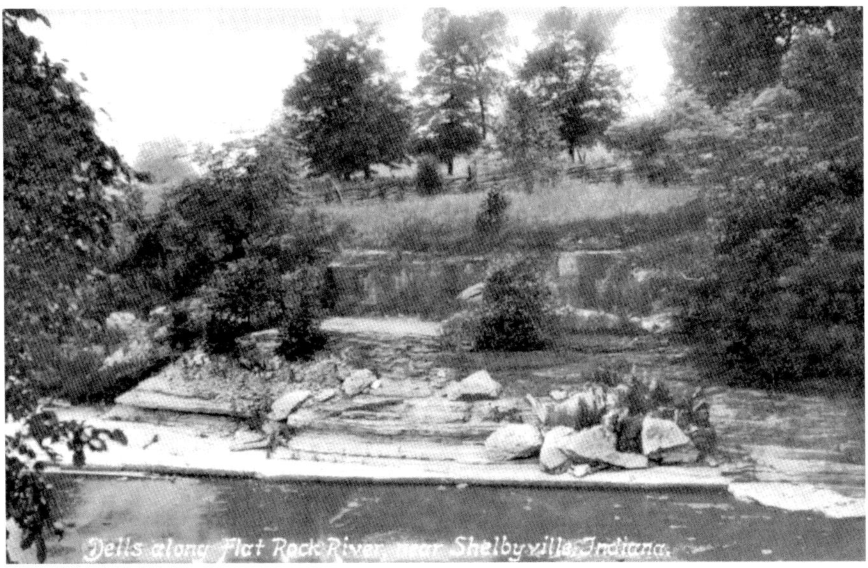

A vintage shot of the Dells along Flat Rock near Shelbyville. Flat Rock is a literal translation of the Indian name *Pack-op-ka.*

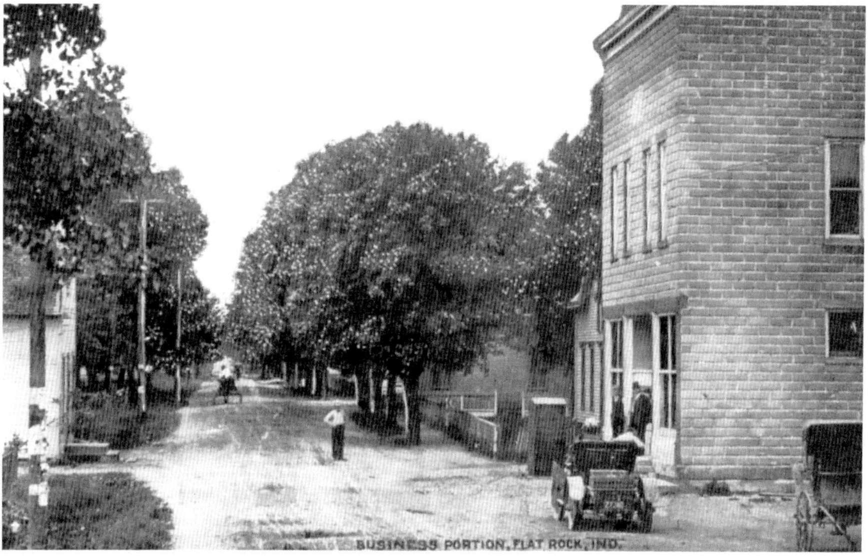

An early twentieth-century postcard of the business portion of Flat Rock. Charles Trimmel wrote that, thanks to the railway influence, Flat Rock thrived more than other communities in the area.

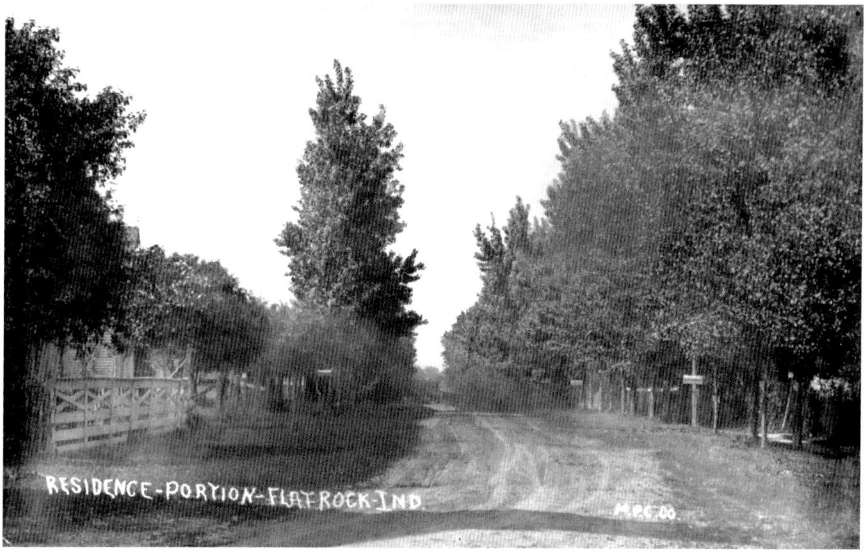

A postcard depicting the residential portion of Flat Rock. In the postcard, one can see the dust kicked up from the dirt roads.

attractive place for residents to settle and establish businesses of their own. In 1853, Jacob Girton arrived and created the Girton Grist and Flouring Mill. The Ohio native didn't stop there; he also managed to create a sawmill, which was operated by a man named Clayton before the establishment was abandoned in 1875.

While there were a number of log cabins in the area, the town itself wasn't laid out with forty-two lots until 1855. Mr. Wooley was the mastermind behind the development of the Flat Rock area. Wooley ended up becoming quite the prominent citizen in the area, selling the land he purchased in 1831 to the C&S Railroad Company. He was also the second postmaster in the community and ran a general store for years. Wooley also was behind the establishment of the Flat Rock Cemetery in 1855.

Jacob Ropp Sr. was another early resident. He moved from Butler County, Ohio, in 1843 to the Flat Rock area, quickly making the acquaintance of Mr. Wooley, who asked the brick mason to build him a house. Ropp ended up building three brick houses, including the Blades house and the Porter home, in addition to the Wooley home.

Charles Trimmel wrote extensively about the establishment of Flat Rock and said that, thanks to the railway influence, the town thrived more than others in the area. He wrote:

> *One of the most important businesses was the grain elevator and warehouse operated by John and Wm. Nading. Wesley Nading and C.P. Isley had general stores and a good trade. Alvin Moore owned a saw mill which he operated several years with a profit. Others in business were Leonard Almeroth and Joseph Conger, blacksmiths, Sidney Conger was a breeder of fine poultry, John Higgins a notary republic, J.C. Keiber, shoemaker, J.R. Leatherman, railroad agent, L. Tice wagonmaker, John White carpenter and early physicians were D.A. Pettigrew and H.M. Connelly, followed by Drs. Norris, Free, Benham, Kennedy, Lytle, Handy and Jones.*

Like many of the other areas, the first schools in Flat Rock were subscription schools with rudimentary buildings that were heated by nothing more than large fireplaces. Trimmel said that the first frame schoolhouse was "built in a lot owned by C.P. Isely in 1845." It was eventually moved to a location near the railroad, where the Parks family lived for many years. In 1861, the first brick schoolhouse arrived on the scene, but it was torn down in 1881. A new building was constructed in 1893. It was made from brick and contained grades one through eight.

In the early part of the twentieth century, it was decided to add two years of high school to the curriculum. Other high school grades were added until, in the 1920s, a complete four-year high school curriculum was finally established in the Flat Rock community. The first class to graduate from the four-year high school was in 1926, though the expansion of the building to accommodate the new high school students wasn't completed until a year later.

"In the fall of 1958, after the Southern Consolidated School building was completed, the Junior and Senior high school students were moved from Flat Rock, leaving grades one through six. In 1977 a new Southwestern Elementary school building was completed and the last day of school in Flat Rock was May 26, 1977," wrote Trimmel.

Early educational buildings also doubled as worship spaces on the weekend. Trimmel said that the Little Ebenezer Church, built in 1852, served as both a schoolhouse and a church. For a long time, churches exclusively held their meetings in school buildings, but in 1875, the United Methodist Church was completed, and the congregation began meeting at that location. The church was named Warner's Chapel after Martin Warner, a major benefactor of the building through a legacy he left after his death. In 1886, it was decided that the name would be changed to Flat Rock United Methodist Church. The Christian Church was founded two years later with nineteen members.

The Flat Rock Hotel was another prominent addition to the community. Established in 1879 by George Hildebrand, the hotel was operated by George as well as his daughter. Other early businesses included a post office and a physician's office operated by Dr. Edward Wertz, who came to Flat Rock after practicing medicine in Shelbyville. According to Trimmel, Wertz "practiced here until his death January 1, 1927. He was followed by Dr. C.R. Walters and his death left a vacancy that was filled by Dr. John A. Davis. He and his wife, Margaret (Jones) Davis located here in 1934. He practiced here until he retired on December 5, 1977, after serving the community for a total of 43 years."

During the Depression era, Flat Rock continued to have flourishing businesses, including a hardware store operated by Roy Nading, a grocery store, a barbershop, garages, blacksmith facilities, a shoe shop and others. Trimmel said that the Flat Rock canning factory, which closed in 1953, was owned and operated by Walter Coulston and John Donnelly. A dance hall, Porter's Camp, that was located just west of Flat Rock offered plenty of amusements, and cottages could be leased.

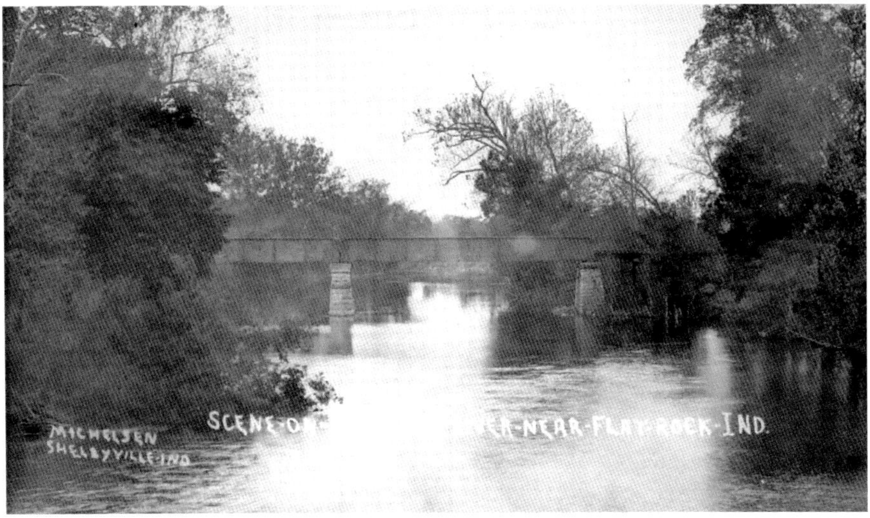

A river postcard taken near Flat Rock, Indiana. The community was known for having flourishing businesses, even during the Great Depression era.

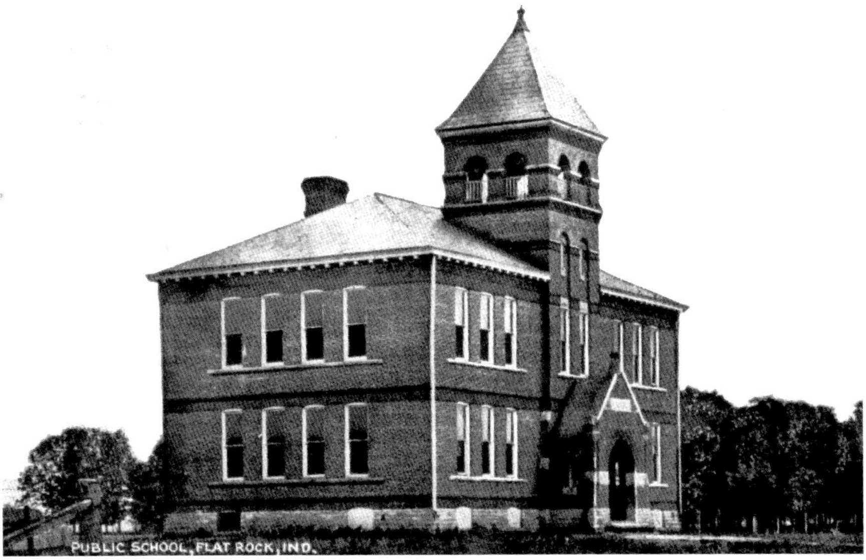

The public school in Flat Rock. According to Charles Trimmel, the early educational buildings in Flat Rock doubled as churches on the weekends.

Trimmel also wrote about the small village of Bynum that was located on the north side of Flat Rock in 1840. Named for William B. Bynum, who was a congressman, one of the more notable establishments in the village consisted of a three-story mill "powered by two water-wheels, one for grinding corn and the other for the five-roller process to grind the wheat for flour. The Bones operated the mill until about 1870 or 1872 when it was sold to Leander Nelson. They made a fine grade of flour, some of which was hauled to Flat Rock by horse and wagon and shipped to other places by train. A Christian Church group met in a room in the mill following the Civil War."

Norristown

Originally called Winterrowd, Norristown was founded on November 22, 1851, with fifty-four lots, platted by David Winterrowd, William P. Winterrowd, Joseph Winterrowd and Henry Deiwert. With a post office and a merchant, the town eventually became established, but the longest surviving store in the community was Orpha Scripture grocery. In addition, Norristown had a barbershop, a blacksmith shop and a creamery that delivered dairy products to the residents of the community.

"An attraction early in the century was a 90-foot long skating rink. The building was located on the south side of the main street. After the white brick school building burned in 1912 or 1913, partitions were put in it and used for a school. It was crowded and some area students were sent to Flat Rock until the red brick building was built on the hill in 1914," wrote Trimmel.

Norristown also had a cemetery that was about a quarter of an acre. It was originally established in 1830 on the farm of Joseph Winterrowd. The cemetery was expanded in 1880, at the same time that the first church was established in the area. The Union Church was a facility that was utilized by a number of denominations, and it has also been known as the Community Church.

A brick schoolhouse was erected in Norristown in 1879. The building was expanded in 1900 with a second story. While the building was used for many years, it was officially closed in 1942, and the students were transferred over to Flat Rock. Eventually, the former school building was demolished.

"A Wesleyan Methodist Church was established and a building was erected and dedicated in December 1891. It was struck by lightning and burned to the ground on August 1, 1934. Later on that year a new building was built. In 1968 the Wesleyan Methodist and Pilgrim Holiness Churches united and became the Wesleyan Church," Trimmel wrote.

Other Communities

Mount Auburn was established in 1837 and platted by John Warner, Christopher Allen, Daniel Allen and William Records. The community had thirty-two lots and was originally named Black Hawk for an Indian warrior. The first merchant in the area was Mr. Huffman, and in 1839, Joseph Hageman established a sawmill. A "corn cracker" was added in 1841, though most would call it a flour mill. A tannery was also located nearby.

These smaller communities, whether or not they still exist today, were all vibrant towns and villages in Shelby County. There were grocery stores, post offices and a number of small businesses that reached out to the residents of these areas. Waldron was originally called Stroupsville for George Stroup, who initially laid out the area in 1854. Waldron contained twenty-four lots and was situated on the Liberty Railroad in the heart of a farming community. George Wooden served as the pioneer merchant in Waldron, operating a general store. There was also an extensive sawmill and

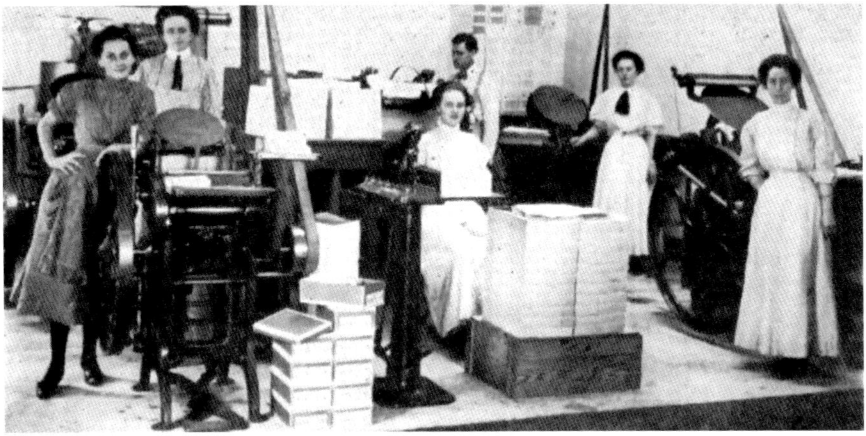

An early 1900s postcard of the press room at the J.H. Meloy Company, a stationer and printer in Waldron, Indiana. Note the number of working women at the company.

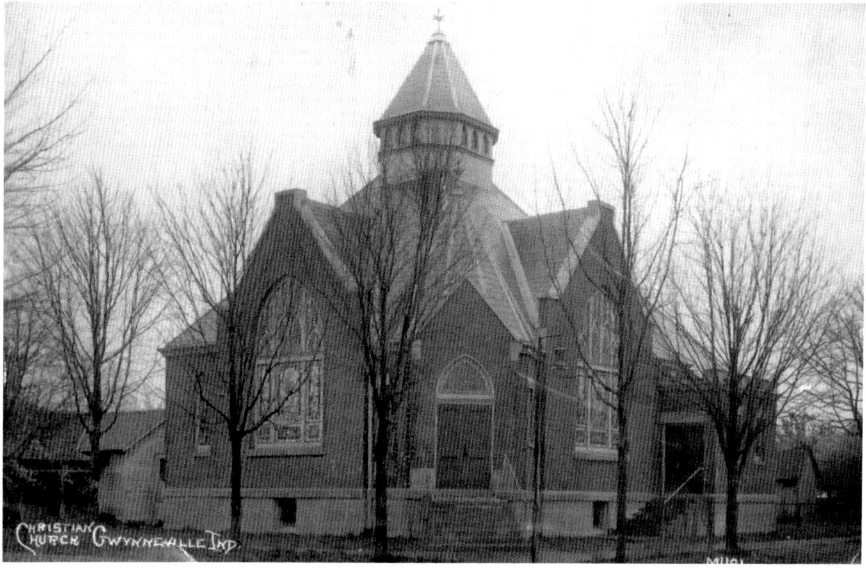

The Christian Church in Gwynneville. As buildings changed, more Gothic Revival architecture began to crop up in places of worship. This is characterized by the long lines and pointed archways.

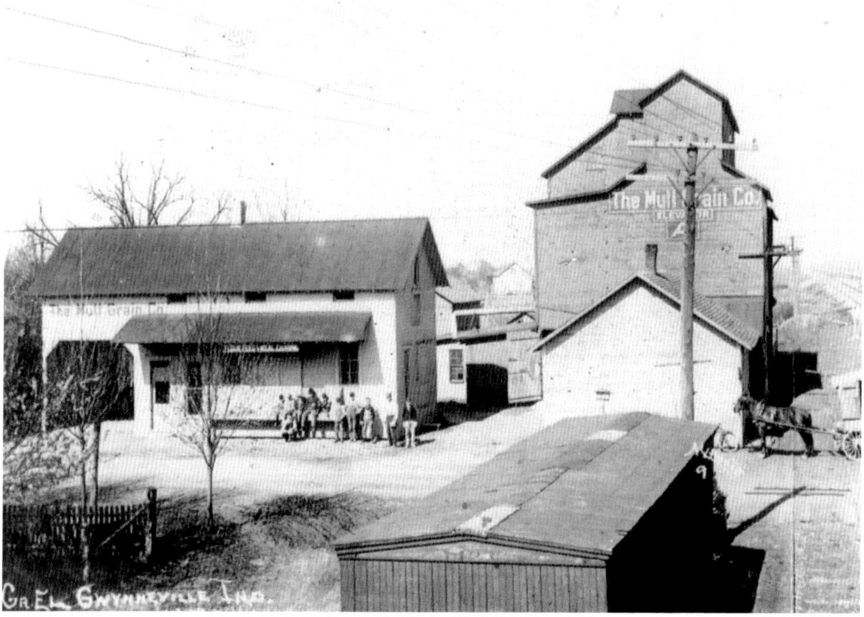

A vintage photograph of the Mull Grain Company in Gwynneville. Note the elevator employees sitting on the porch waiting for a delivery. *Courtesy of Donna Tracy at the Blue Bird Restaurant.*

gristmill in the area, in addition to a number of other businesses such as a grocery store, dry goods shop, restaurant, millinery shop, harness business and poultry yard.

Waldron is unique because it happened to be sitting on top of a natural gas dome, which was tapped to provide gas to the residents of the town for cooking and lighting.

Gwynneville was platted by Alex Pollitt in 1881 and named for merchant and businessman O'Brien Gwynne, who lived in Rush County. Warren King was the first merchant in Gwynneville, and the community was known for its tile and brick production, in addition to its natural gas wells. Some of the other entities in the area included the Gwynneville Christian Church and the Mullin Grain Company.

The Gwynneville School, opened in 1886, was known as the Dormer School. When it closed, it was replaced by a one-room building in 1918, but it too closed, and the children who attended there were assigned to the Morristown school district.

Chapter 8

FAMOUS SHELBY COUNTY RESIDENTS

Like any other area of the state, Shelby County has several notables who have made their mark, not only locally but also nationally and beyond, with their unique gifts and talents. Whether the world's oldest or tallest or a celebrated actor or writer, Shelby County has been home to all at one time or another. Here are a few of the more famous members of the Shelby County community.

Politics as Usual

Indiana has had its share of important political leaders, but in Shelby County, Thomas Hendricks is one worth noting. Hendricks was born near East Fultonham, Ohio, on September 7, 1819. His father, William Hendricks (governor of Indiana from 1822 to 1825), moved the family to Indiana in 1820, convinced that they would be prosperous in the new state. Originally living on a farmstead in Madison, the Hendricks moved to Shelby County in 1822. William became fairly wealthy as a farmer, operated a general store and became involved in local politics. This influenced young Thomas early on.

Well educated for the time, Thomas Hendricks began his studies in the local common school and then attended Hanover College in 1841. He studied law in Chambersburg, Pennsylvania, before eventually returning

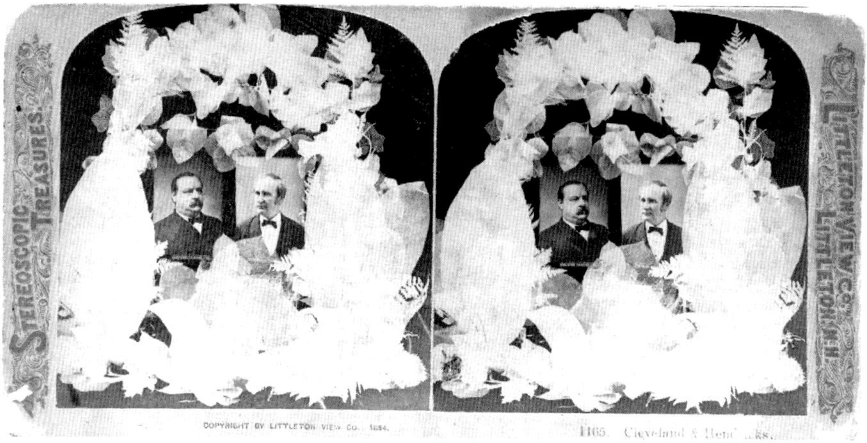

A campaign "stereo" postcard of Grover Cleveland and Thomas Hendricks. Hendricks, a Shelby County native, was elected vice president but died shortly afterward.

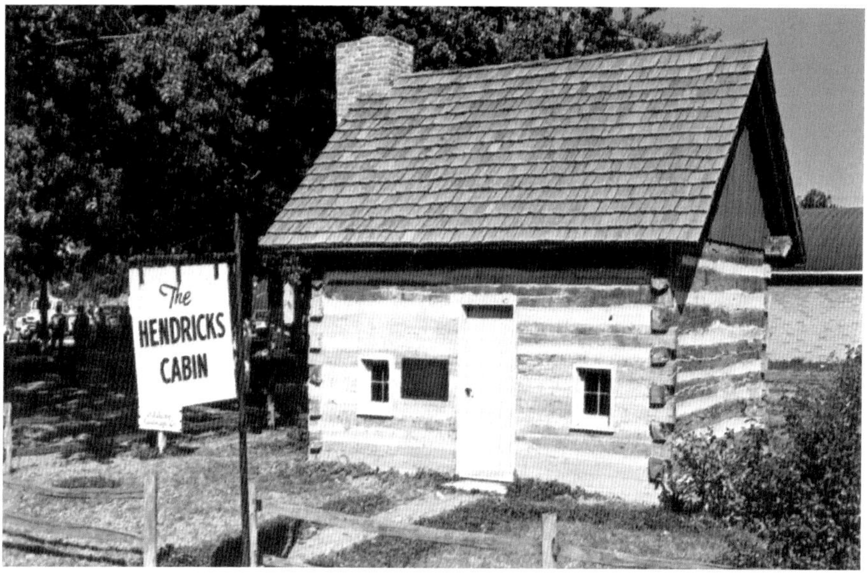

Thomas Hendricks's cabin, which is located near the Shelby County Fairgrounds. Not unlike President Lincoln, Hendricks was born in very rudimentary circumstances. *Courtesy of the Grover Museum.*

to Shelby County, where he worked in the law office of Stephen Major. On September 26, 1845, Hendricks married Eliza Morgan after a two-year courtship. The couple had one son, Morgan, who was born on January 16, 1848, but sadly, he died at the age of three.

In 1848, Thomas became a member of the Indiana State House of Representatives, serving only one term. He was elected Speaker of the House in the 1849 session. He also served as a delegate to the Indiana constitutional convention in 1851 while serving as a member of Congress (which he was elected to in 1850). During his term as a congressman, he was the chairman of the Committee on Mileage as well as the Committee on Invalid Pensions. His support for an unpopular bill on the extension of slavery led to his defeat when he sought reelection. After leaving the halls of Congress, Hendricks served as commissioner of the General Land Office, appointed by President Franklin Pierce.

Afterward, he returned to Shelby County, where he attempted a run for governor of Indiana but failed in that bid. He returned to the practice of law until his election, by the Indiana General Assembly, to the United States Senate in 1863.

He finally won his bid for Indiana governor on his third try in 1872. He was the first Democratic governor elected in the North after the Civil War. Hendricks had the unfortunate job of running the state during the economic panic of 1973, which resulted in unemployment, failed businesses, multiple worker strikes and the bottoming out of farm prices. He even had to utilize the state's militia on two occasions in order to end strikes. It is well established that Hendricks was loyal to the Union throughout the Civil War, but he was opposed to the Reconstruction program imposed on the South after the war. He tended to sympathize with white supremacists in the South and opposed all legislation aimed at assisting freedmen, according to the *Britannica Concise Encyclopedia*.

As governor, one of Hendricks's notable laws was the Baxter Bill, which put temperance laws into motion. Unfortunately, the 1873 bill would be rescinded two years later. He also put into place the plans for building a new statehouse, as the old one had become very dilapidated. Aside from those two acts, Hendricks's time as governor was largely uneventful.

It would take Hendricks a couple of tries before he would stand second to the most powerful office in the country. His first run, in 1876, for the office of vice president was as the running mate for Democratic presidential candidate Samuel Tilden. Their ticket won the popular vote, but in a similar result to the Bush/Gore election of 2000, Hendricks and Tilden ended up shy of the electoral votes needed to secure the election. After disputing the election, a commission was established to determine the winner. The commission sided with the Republican Party. Four years later, Hendricks was nominated again for the post of vice president by the Democratic Party, but he had to decline for health reasons.

Finally, the third time would prove to be the charm for the Hoosier. Running on a ticket with Grover Cleveland, Hendricks was elected vice president in 1884. Sadly, his poor health proved to be too much, and he died in his sleep on November 25, 1885, while visiting Indianapolis only a few short months after being inaugurated on March 4, 1885. His funeral was held in St. Paul's Cathedral, Indianapolis, with interment at Crown Hill Cemetery. The office of vice president remained vacant until the election of Levi Morton in 1888 and his subsequent inauguration in 1889.

Thomas A. Hendricks's lasting claim to fame is that he remains the only U.S. vice president (who was never also a president) to appear on U.S. currency: the ten-dollar "tombstone" silver certificate of 1886. The border outlining the portrait of Hendricks resembled a tombstone, thus accounting for the unique nickname for the certificate.

A "Major" Literary Influence

If James Whitcomb Riley is the most well-known Hoosier poet, then Charles Major and his literary offerings are not far behind. Born on July 25, 1856, to a middle-class family in Indianapolis (though they relocated to Shelbyville

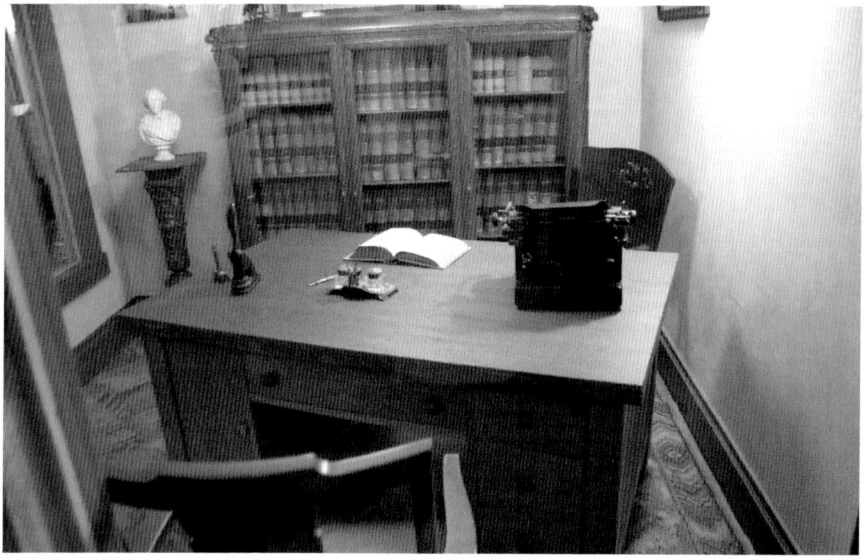

Charles Major's desk, which is on display at the Grover Museum's "Step Back in Time" exhibit. Major was not only an attorney but a notable writer as well. *Author's private collection.*

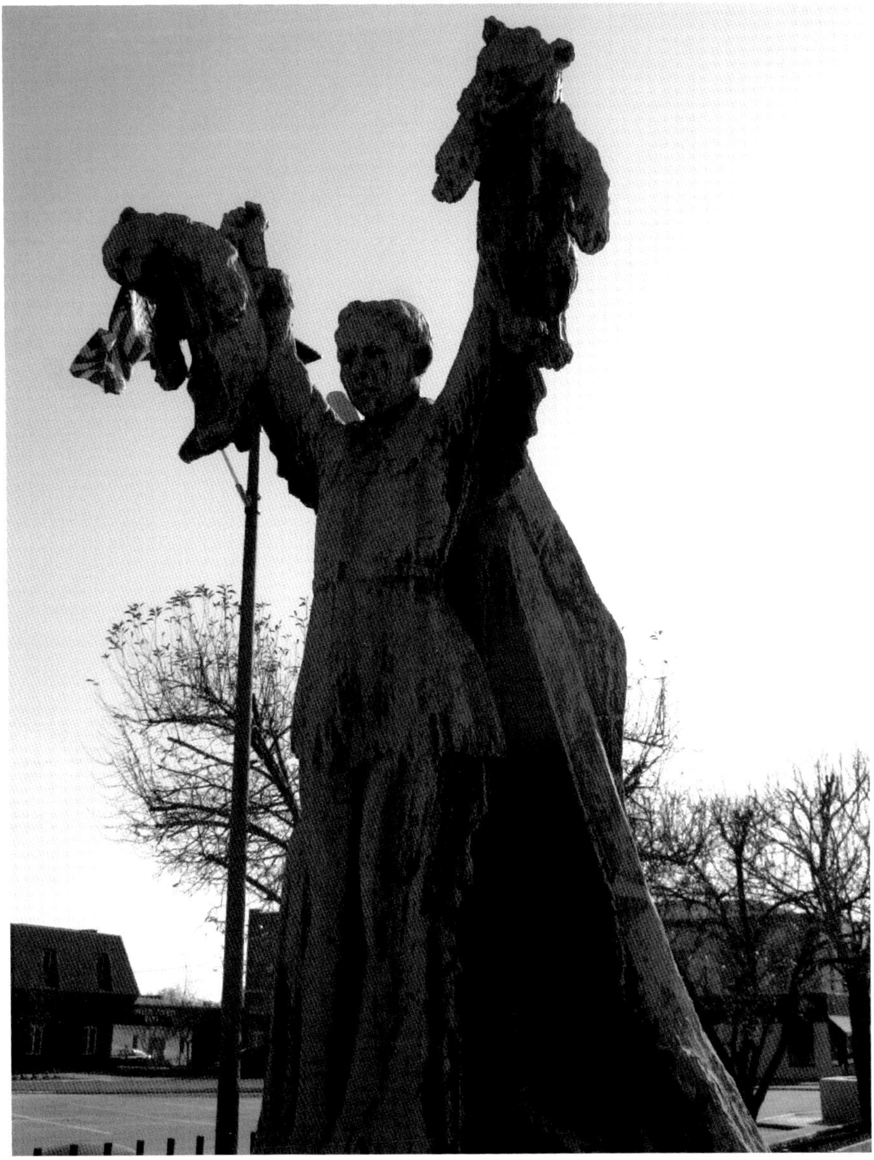

Major's most famous character, Balsar, the hero of *The Bears of Blue River*, has a statue erected to him on the Public Square in downtown Shelbyville. *Author's private collection.*

when Major was thirteen), Major developed an interest in law and English history at an early age.

He attended the University of Michigan and was admitted to the Indiana Bar in 1877. Major returned to Shelbyville, where he opened a law practice and gave his political ambitions a whirl with a term in the state legislature.

Still, his passion for writing was unabated, and in 1898 his first novel, *When Knighthood Was in Flower*, was published. The historical romance was a huge hit and even landed on the *New York Times* bestseller list. Stage and film adaptations would follow, but it was enough for Major to know that his writing talent was worth exploring.

As his career as an author took off, Major concentrated more of his efforts on his writings rather than his law career, and in 1899, he closed the practice. His second novel, *Dorothy Vernon of Haddon Hall*, was another hit, and the eventual film based on the book starred screen legend Mary Pickford.

To Hoosiers, Charles Major will always be best remembered for his stories set in Shelby County along the Big Blue River. *The Bears of Blue River* and *Uncle Tom Andy Bill: A Story of Bears and Indian Treasure*, published in 1901 and 1908, respectively, are adventure novels that tell the story of young Balser Brent and Tom Andy Bill Addison, who are always up for adventure, wild animals and getting out of tight spaces and dangerous situations. For many Hoosiers, *The Bears of Blue River* is mandatory reading.

The third book of the Shelby County trilogy, *A Forest Hearth: A Romance of Indiana in the Thirties* (1905), is a sentimental love story set on the banks of the Blue River and concerns the courting of Rita, but Major continued to set his work against a vivid backdrop of Indiana landscape.

"In his novels, Charles Major provides a colorful picture of the early landscape in Indiana and insight into the mindset of pioneers concerning their natural surroundings," said a Ball State University website dedicated to the land and literature of the state.

Sadly, Major died of liver cancer on February 13, 1913, but his work has been immortalized with a statue of Balser Brent holding up two bear cubs on the Public Square in Shelbyville. The Grover Museum has Major's desk on display in its "town," and each year people in the county and from surrounding areas descend on Shelbyville for the Bears of Blue River Festival, which features a parade, entertainment, food and fun for all.

The Minister's Daughter

Anyone who has watched one of the Ma and Pa Kettle films—*Meet Me in St. Louis* with Judy Garland or *the Long, Long Trailer* with Lucille Ball and

Desi Arnez—has been touched by the comedic genius of character actress Marjorie Main.

Main was born Mary Tomlinson on February 24, 1890, in Acton. Her father was a minister who didn't approve of the theatre or any kind of dramatic aspirations that his daughter enjoyed. She attended Franklin College and eventually wanted to study drama at Hamilton College in Kentucky. Her father agreed to this educational plan provided that Mary become a teacher, which she did for a year before joining the Chautaugua circuit. The troupe had a Shakespeare company, and one of her first roles was as Katherine in *The Taming of the Shrew*. Her father reportedly was fine with the role, as it was classical theatre. For her performance, she received eight dollars a week.

Main made her way to New York City, but the competition led her to a stock company in Fargo, North Dakota, and ultimately the vaudeville stage. It was during this stint that Tomlinson changed her name to Marjorie Main, reasoning that it was an easy name to remember and the anonymity wouldn't cause her family any embarrassment.

In 1921, she married Stanley Krebs, a minister and psychologist, who was a writer and could often be found on the lecture circuit. He was twenty-six years older than Main, and after their wedding, the couple traveled together while Krebs lectured. According to sources, Main called this the happiest time of her life. When Krebs's work kept him based in New York, Main returned to the stage, working with some of the greats of the business, including Pauline Lord, Ethel Barrymore, Mae West and Barbara Stanwick.

Krebs died in 1935, and as a result, Main threw herself into her work. She landed her first Broadway role in the show *Dead End*. Main repeated her celebrated performance of the slum mother in the movie adaptation, which starred legendary actor Humphrey Bogart. The part earned her praise from the public, the critics and the film industry. From then on, other roles followed, and she became a contract player for MGM Studios.

One of her more memorable roles was her performance in *The Women* with Wallace Beery. The teaming was so popular that the couple was reunited in *Barnacle*, which was also well received by the public, though privately, the actors didn't always get along well, and Main wasn't happy about being half of a duo. She also didn't like Beery's habit of ad-libbing on the set.

Main hardly fit the profile of the typical Hollywood star. Though she lived in Los Angeles and at one point actually purchased a car, she preferred to ride the bus to work and initially lived in an apartment before buying a small bungalow near the MGM studio. She took her meals in the studio cafeteria rather than "lunching" with the bigwigs at places such as the Brown Derby. She even spent many of her evenings people-watching in the park. It was those observations that would serve her well in the character roles she took, and a lot of her success came from her acting in supporting roles to other big stars such as Clark Gable or Robert Taylor. She did have a few starring roles, but they weren't as well known by the moviegoing public.

Main came to the role that would define her career when MGM loaned her to Paramount for the movie *Murder, He Says* with Fred MacMurray. In it, Main played the role of a hillbilly woman trying to keep her unruly kids under control. The brilliant comedic performance was a hit, and according to Jim Hicks, who runs a website dedicated to Main, she pulled out all the stops for this part.

"Fred MacMurray gave a brilliant performance and Marjorie matched him all the way," he writes. "She pulled out screen exhibiting no restraint at all. Her voice ranges from whiny purr to a raucous bellow. She never gave a wilder or funnier performance on the screen."

It was that performance that led film executives to cast her in *The Egg and I*, the story of a young married couple who become chicken farmers. Main played the role of "Ma Kettle" opposite Percy Kilbride's "Pa." The characters were so well liked by the public that a spinoff was planned, and the result were several "Kettle" movies.

Main wasn't overly enthusiastic about the role at first, but she eventually warmed to the character and found a way to take her evenings of observation and put them to good use. She took pride in creating her own wardrobe and even added lines of dialogue. According to Hicks, she closely watched scripts and was quick to eschew anything that was antithetical to her personal convictions. "She refused to play a scene in one film which called for Ma Kettle to be slightly tipsy. She later claimed that she refused because her grandmother was one of the founders of the Women's Christian Temperance Union," Hicks wrote.

Unlike the teaming with Beery, Main got along famously with Kilbride and was quoted as saying that he was the "best dead-pan actor in the business."

The Kettle films ended in 1957, and other than the occasional appearance on television, Main kept to her simple life of cleaning, cooking and watching her old friends on television in old movies. For the most part, she had retired from acting.

On April 10, 1975, Main died of cancer at St. Vincent's Hospital in Los Angeles. She was buried at the famous Forest Lawn Cemetery, where she had had her husband's remains reinterred in 1954.

Age Is Relative

If you are only as old as you feel, then everyone should enjoy a long and happy life like Edna Ruth Parker. Parker was born on a farm near Bengal in Hendricks Township on April 20, 1893, during an economic depression. She was raised on traditional farm foods, such as meat and starch items, and after graduating from Franklin High School, she went on to Franklin College, where she obtained her teaching certificate.

Parker's first assignment was in a two-room schoolhouse in Smithland, but that tenure ended when she married her next-door neighbor, Earl Parker, in 1913. They had two sons, Earl Jr. and Clifford, but Earl Sr. died in 1939, and Edna Parker would ultimately end up outliving her children as well.

Edna Ruth Parker lived alone on a farm on Blue Ridge Road from the time she was 45 to the age of 100. At that time, despite being in good health, she moved in with one of her sons. According to one story, one night after returning from a basketball game, Parker's son and his wife found Parker lying unconscious in the backyard. She was only visible because she was wearing a red sweater. The family worried that she might die, but Parker made a full recovery, having suffered only some minor injuries. She moved into the Heritage House Convalescent Center retirement community at the age of 114.

Parker enjoyed a variety of activities, including reading and reciting poetry from favorite writers such as James Whitcomb Riley, and she would recite pieces to anyone who visited her. She was a fan of the daily newspaper, and she received cards from an ever-growing list of well-wishers. She even sent autographs to people who would write to her and ask for one. According to Wikipedia, "In 2007, she received a letter from President George W. Bush on her 114th birthday, who thanked her for 'sharing her wisdom and experiences with younger generations.' Also at that time, she was given the key to the city of Shelbyville from the Mayor, and was visited by the state Governor and Senator." On August 13, 2007, Edna Parker was recognized as the world's oldest woman following the death of Japan's Yone Minigawa. She is one of only twenty-one people who have been validated to have lived to be 115 years of age.

Edna Ruth Parker died in her nursing home on November 26, 2008, and is buried in Shelbyville's Miller Cemetery. After her death, the "world's oldest woman" title went to Maria de Jesus in Portugal.

The Lord of the Jungle

Born on August 8, 1900, in Freedom, Indiana, "Big" James Pierce first made a name for himself as an all-American on the Indiana University football team. After graduating from the Big Ten University in 1921, he moved westward and began coaching, taking on small acting jobs in his spare time.

Of course, silent movies were the cinematic offerings at the time, and in 1923, Pierce scored a role in *The Deerslayer*, which prompted him to move to California. There, he divided his time between his movie commitments and his coaching duties at Glendale High School, where one of his players was then-unknown John Wayne.

A chance meeting with Edgar Rice Burroughs at a party for his daughter Joan led to Pierce landing the role of a lifetime when Burroughs insisted that Pierce appear in the next Tarzan movie, *Tarzan and the Golden Lion*. Pierce realized that roles such as this didn't come along every day, and he quickly backed out of his commitment to play a role in *Wings* (which eventually starred Gary Cooper) in order to don a loincloth and assume the role of the Lord of the Jungle.

The silent film was a huge hit, but in addition to playing Tarzan, Pierce also fell in love with Joan Burroughs, who agreed to marry the actor. The couple tied the knot on his twenty-eighth birthday, and they voiced the roles of Tarzan and Jane for many radio programs. After his role as Tarzan, Pierce acted in several westerns, as well as a *Flash Gordon* motion picture serial in which he played Prince Thun, a trusted friend of Flash.

Pierce served as a pilot during World War II in the National Airmen's Reserve, which was the forerunner to the Air National Guard. "Big" James Pierce died on December 11, 1983, and he and Joan are buried in Shelbyville's Forest Hills Cemetery, where their tombstones bear the names of their cinematic counterparts, Tarzan and Jane.

Mr. Basketball

When it comes to a sports distinction, William "Bill" Garrett has one of the highest honors the state can bestow. His life in Shelbyville began on April 4, 1929, and he would become the first African American to play in Big Ten basketball.

After playing for Shelbyville High School and being named "Mr. Basketball" in 1947, Garrett attended Indiana University, where he was the first African American to regularly play for the Hoosier team. Not only that, but he was also the school's leading scorer and rebounder. He was also voted by his teammates as IU's most valuable player. Still, there were tensions off the court for Garrett as he had to struggle with discrimination and tense racial relations. Undeterred, he made all-American in 1951 and was snapped up by the Boston Celtics in the second round of the draft. He was only the third African American ever to be drafted by a professional club.

However, his two-year service with the army proved to kill the basketball career he envisioned in Boston, and he was cut from the team. Garrett then played for the famed Harlem Globetrotters before returning to Indiana, where he coached at Crispus Attucks High School in Indianapolis.

In addition, Garrett also served as the assistant dean of student services at IUPUI. He died in 1974, the same year that he was inducted into the Indiana Basketball Hall of Fame, and he is buried in Crown Hill Cemetery.

In 2008, Indiana University renamed a gymnasium in memory of Garrett. The gym was previously associated with Ora Wildermuth, a trustee who was utterly opposed to integration in the 1940s. According to the *Chicago Tribune*'s Rex W. Huppke, some felt that Wildermuth's name should have been removed entirely from the building, but Ed Marshall, IU's vice-president for diversity, says that the combination of names provides an educational bridge for people. "We realize there were some negative moments in our history, we can't deny that, we can't make that go away," says Marshall. "But we can use that point in time to educate current and future generations about the lack of validity of those views."

The university not only changed the name of the building but also installed a plaque outside of the gym outlining the purpose of combining these two names. Tom Graham, author of *Getting Open*, a book about Garrett, said in the *Tribune* article that he was happy with the decision to incorporate both names on the gym.

"That gives credence to the explanation that they view this as a teaching opportunity about the evolution of racial attitudes," Graham said. "Had they simply taken Wildermuth's name off the building, that contention would have lingered and it would have detracted a bit from the addition of Garrett's name."

Life Is Short…I'm Not

While there have been many "big" and important people in Shelby County, one person stands head and shoulders above the rest: Sandy Allen. The "giantess" of Shelbyville was born on June 18, 1955, as a "normal" baby, weighing six pounds, five ounces, but there was also a tumor on her pituitary gland that released a growth hormone and caused her to grow at an accelerated rate. By the time she was ten, she was already literally at the head of the class, at six feet, three inches, towering above everyone else—including the teacher.

Allen underwent an operation for her acromeglay, or "giant's disease," when she was twenty-two in order to stop the continued growth of her body. Her final height would be an impressive seven feet, seven and a quarter inches. As she often put it, "Life is short...I'm not."

Still, life was far from easy for Allen, who experienced more than her fair share of teasing from the other children in her class. She recalled a graduation party during her sixth grade year that was held at a local skating rink. Due to the size of her feet, the rink could not accommodate her with skates, and she was unable to participate.

"I just wanted to be like other girls," she said to Buck Wolf. "They called me beanpole, a monster and a freak. And that's what they said to my face. I can only imagine what they said behind my back…You can laugh off some of the jokes, but how many times do you want to hear 'How's the weather up there?' especially if they are being mean about it. Sometimes you want to spit on them and say 'It's raining.'"

That humor in the face of difficult daily struggles is what got Allen through the toughest times, including incidents where she was stuck in a bathtub, had difficulty with everyday tasks and had to find clothes custom made for her.

"Just try washing the dishes when the sink only comes up to your thigh. Try finding a pair of pantyhose that fit. A lot of women complain that they don't have a thing to wear. Those women should talk to me," she said in the interview.

Rita Rose, a personal friend of Allen's and the author of *World's Tallest Woman: The Giantess of Shelbyville High*, said that Allen's one-liners might be a coping mechanism for her challenges, but Allen had comedic timing that would make a seasoned professional applaud. During a friend's wedding, Rose said that Allen admired the beautiful dress worn by the bride and commented wistfully that she would never have a chance to don a wedding gown. The friend suggested that someday, Allen's prince would come. "Well if he does," Allen remarked, "he'd better be eight feet tall and riding a damn elephant!"

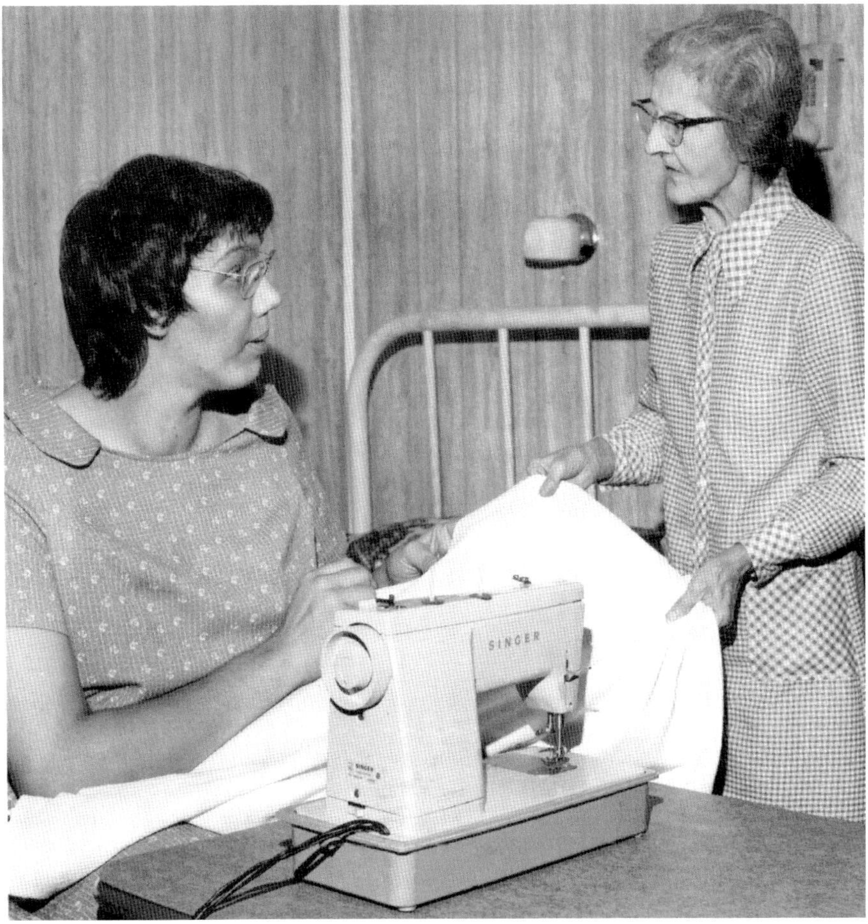

Sandy Allen, the world's tallest woman, and the grandmother who raised her. Sandy was known for saying "Life is short…I'm not." *Courtesy of Rita Rose.*

In 1976, Guinness World Records recognized Allen as the World's Tallest Woman. The moniker suddenly gave her a forum to use her height as an asset. Allen was hounded for personal appearances, which benefitted her financially, as well as helping her create awareness for those with differences. She traveled the world, appearing in Fellini's *Casanova* as well as televised spots on *Oprah*, *The Maury Povich Show*, *The Jerry Springer Show* and even shock jock Howard Stern's radio show. "I don't want to hurt Howard Stern's reputation, but he is actually a nice guy," she said in an interview.

Allen even attracted the attention of the King of Pop, Michael Jackson. During an event for Guinness in San Francisco, Wolf writes that the singer approached Allen and introduced himself. Convinced that he was not really

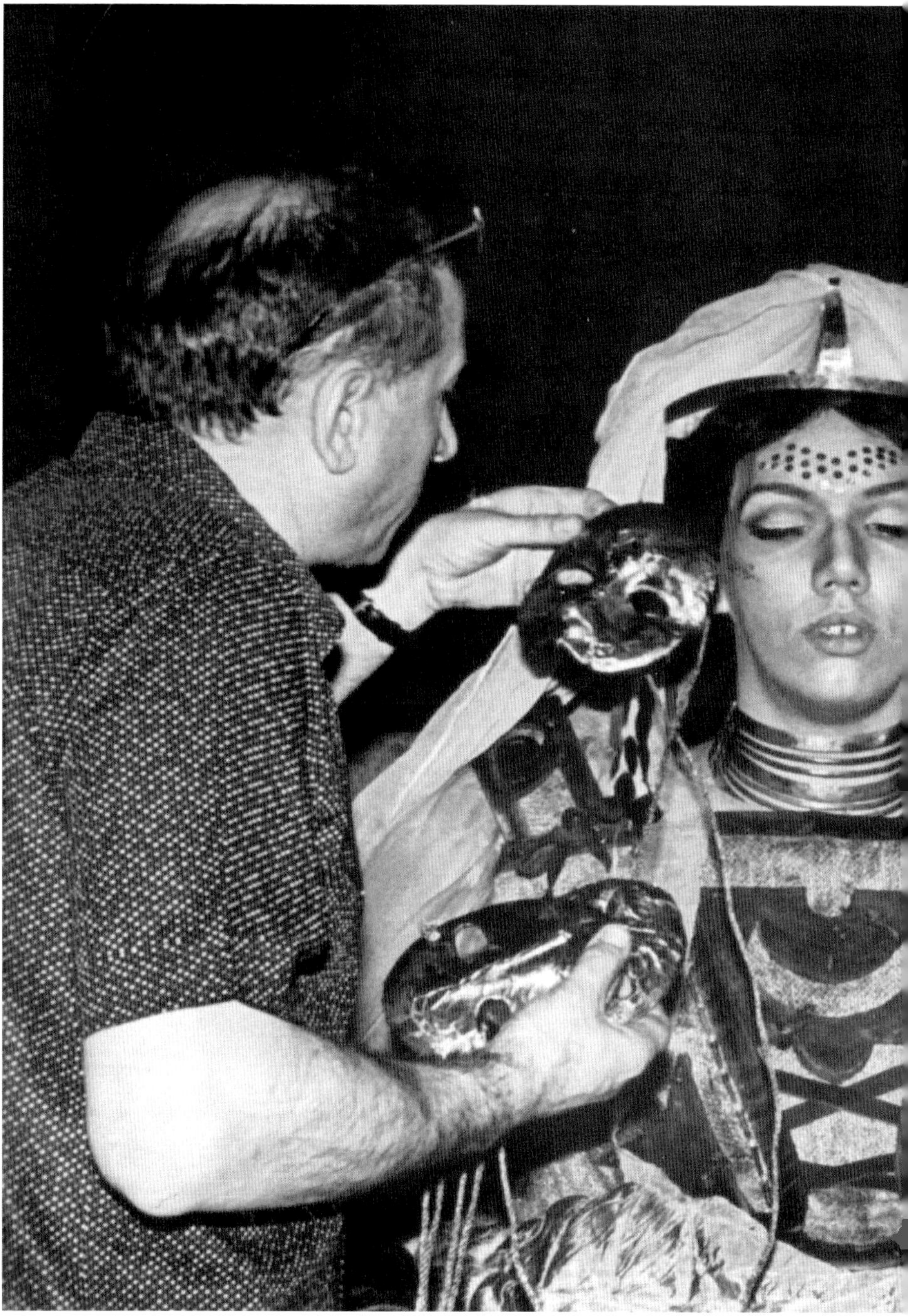

Sandy Allen prepares for her role as a giantess in Fellini's *Casanova*. Over the years, she did many programs for schoolchildren and Guinness and even made the acquaintance of the King of Pop, Michael Jackson. *Courtesy of Rita Rose.*

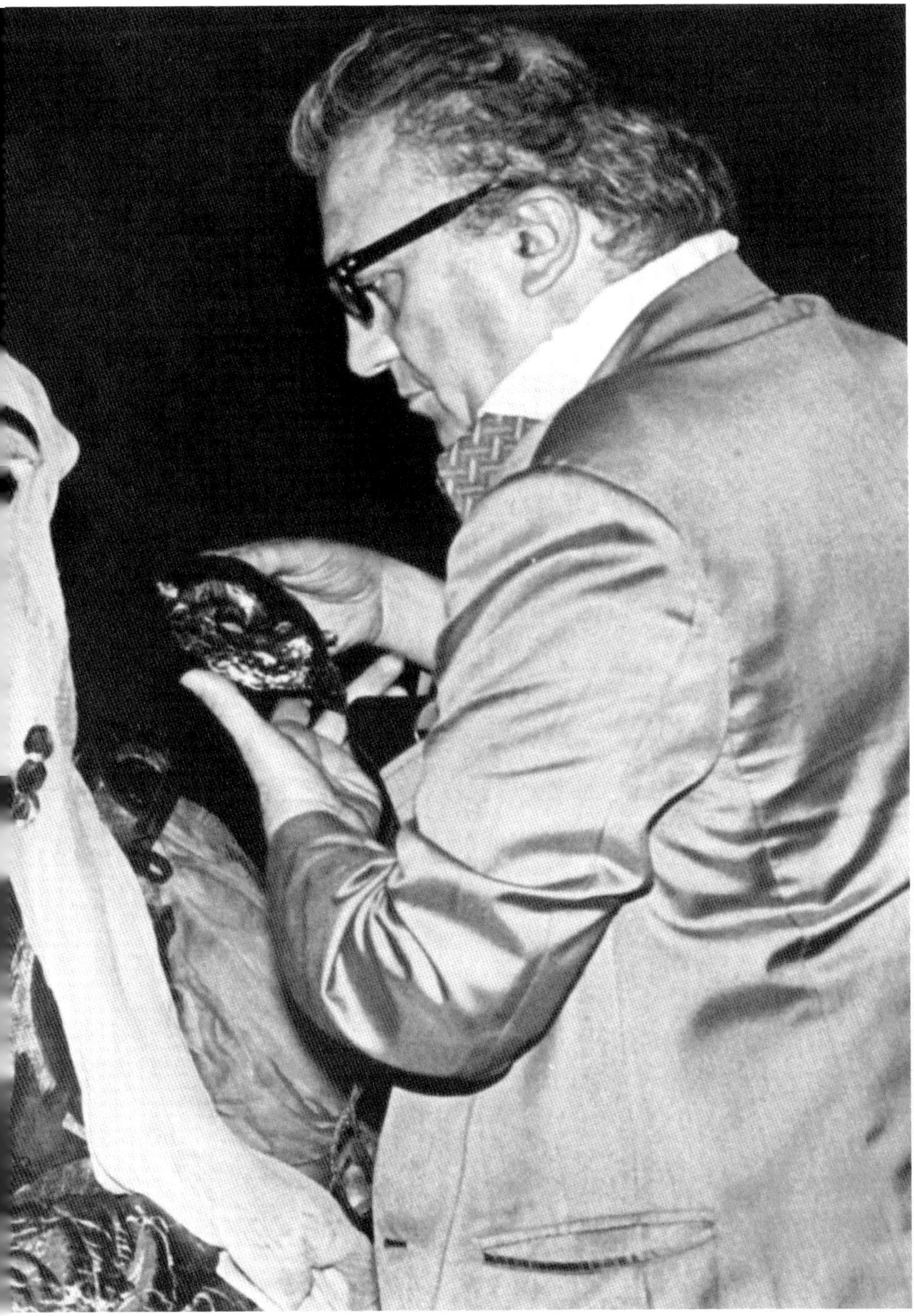

Michael Jackson, she tossed off, "Yeah, sure—and I'm the next president of the United States." It was Jackson, however, and the next day he presented her with signed copies of his albums, and she sent him a copy of the *Guinness Book of World Records* with her name in it. "I was truly impressed with his humble kindness," she said in Wolf's interview. "I still can't believe he sought me out."

Rose said that Allen worked in the Indiana state veterinarian's office and for the City of Indianapolis as a receptionist for Mayor William Hudnut's office and the department of public works, but her real calling came from talking to kids about feeling "different."

Rose wrote, "She was part of the Pacer's Reading Program where she read to elementary school kids and presented a program called 'It's OK to be different' in which she talked about her life, about being an outcast and how important it was for people to have compassion and acceptance to those who don't fit in."

During the presentation, she also brought in a pair of her 22EEE shoes in order to let kids try them on. Rose said that the talk was always warm and inspirational, and even today, she meets those who met Allen who never forgot the experience.

"One reason Sandy liked kids was because they were so honest. She said, 'They come up to me and ask how I got so tall, how much do I eat and how I sit on the toilet. Kids will ask you anything!' The adults, however, would hang back and stare, and it was difficult to engage them in conversation," Rose explained.

In Allen's later years, mobility issues made public speaking difficult, and often she relied on a motorized wheelchair to get around. Throughout her life, she was plagued by a variety of illnesses such as atrophic muscles, diabetes and severe bladder infections.

"Sandy spent the last several years of her life in Indianapolis before moving to the Heritage House Convalescent Center in Shelbyville where she lived with the World's Oldest Living Woman, Edna Parker," Rose said. "She had a private room with her own furniture, computer and other amenities."

There were still a lot of visitors, of course, but Allen was lonely after losing her mobility. Ministers visited Allen, and Rose said she believes that Allen was preparing for the end. She hoped to help Rose promote her book, but she died on August 13, 2008, right after Rose's book was published. Proceeds from the book benefit the Sandy Allen Memorial Fund, which in turn benefits Girls, Inc. of Shelbyville. The fund is administered by the Blue River Community Foundation of Shelbyville.

"She was so thrilled to be remembered for something other than just being tall," said Rose.

Chapter 9

SHELBY COUNTY TODAY

Shelby County remains a community that is as committed to its past as it is to evolving into the future. Though the area is still dotted with farms and many of the family names that were familiar in the 1800s, Shelby County is a region that has the best of both worlds.

Shelby County Historical Society

Established during the county's centennial celebration in 1922, the Shelby County Historical Society was created by a group of enthusiastic citizens who wanted to offer the residents of the county plenty of historical programs that would highlight the rich history of the community. Over time, the enthusiasm and membership dwindled, but in 1951, there was a resurgence of the organization when it became obvious to a group of local history buffs that perhaps some of the old history was being lost forever. They decided that the time had come to reactivate the historical society.

After incorporating in 1957, the society began to hold its annual Blue River Valley Pioneer Craft fair in 1967. This event was held at the fairgrounds in the fall and became a tradition throughout the region. The craft fair includes arts such as wood carving, tatting, basketry, baked goods and soap making.

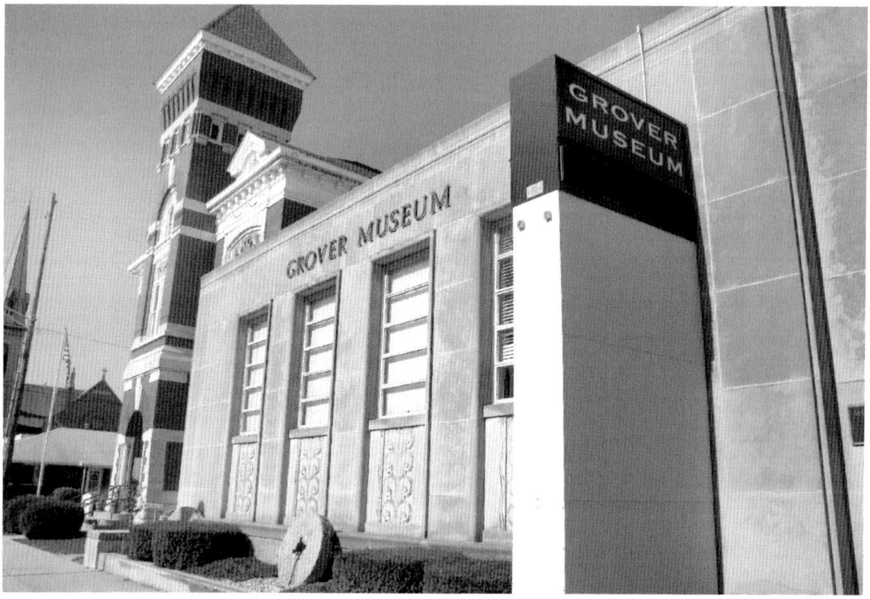

The Grover Museum serves as the home of the Shelby County Historical Society and maintains several permanent collections as well as special displays. *Author's private collection.*

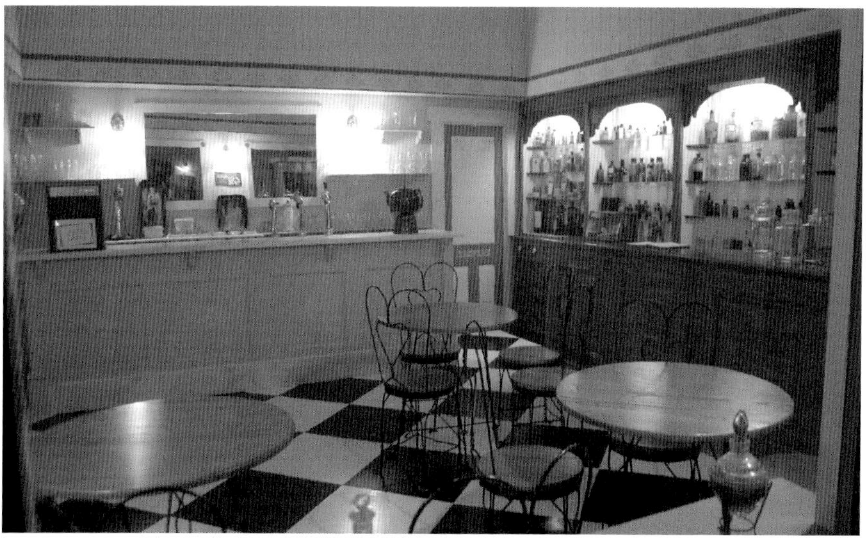

Above and opposite, top: The soda fountain and general store are part of the "Step Back in Time" exhibit, which allows visitors a chance to see what Main Street Shelbyville was like long ago. *Author's private collection.*

Opposite, bottom: The one-room schoolhouse in the Grover Museum. According to director Candace Miller, students studying Indiana history have the chance to hold class in the schoolhouse in order to see what it was like to be a student in the 1800s. *Author's private collection.*

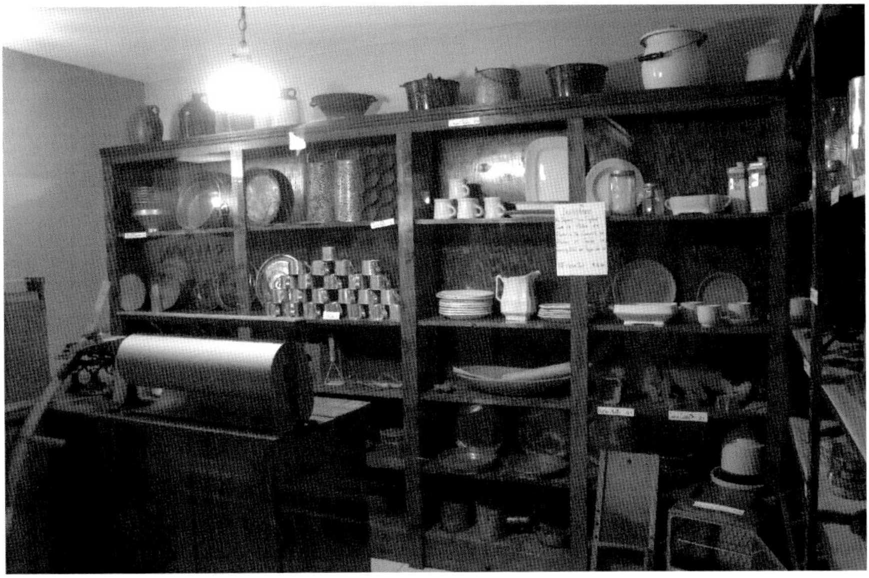

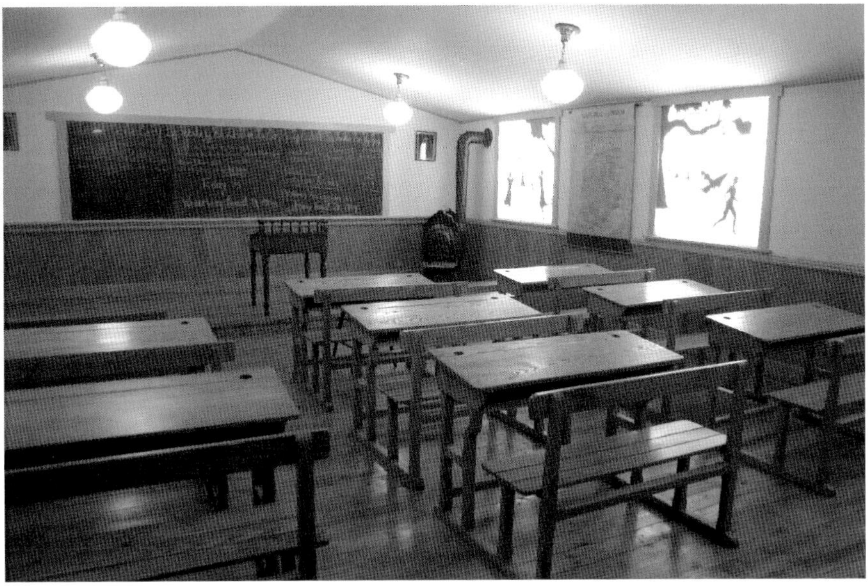

In 1980, the society was able to purchase the Elks building at 52 West Broadway, which is now home to the Grover Museum. Society members donated their time, talent and treasure to creating a museum that reflected the history of the county. In fact, the displays within the building are actually a peek into the past as visitors not only see the photos and memorabilia on exhibit but actually see a recreation of a time that is no more.

The first stop in the Grover Museum's unique display is a re-creation of the old interurban as it might have appeared in 1910. From there, a quaint "town" atmosphere encourages visitors to see the kinds of businesses and shops that the citizens of the county might have frequented in the "good old days." There is a hardware store, a barbershop, an emporium (complete with a soda fountain courtesy of the Coca-Cola Company), a cemetery, a barn, a rudimentary doctor's office, a one-room schoolhouse and a saloon among the displays that take the visitor back to a simpler time and offer a sense of lifestyle, as well as an interactive history lesson.

Genealogy and History House

For those looking to trace their roots, one of the first stops is the Genealogy and History House, a division of the Shelbyville–Shelby County Public Library. Acclaimed as being one of the finest genealogy libraries in the state, a surprising number of people are referred to the Genealogy and History House to begin their search for long lost kin.

"Many people are referred here because of the amount of books that we have, not only for Shelby County, but also for the surrounding counties and other counties throughout the state. We also have a number of books on other states, such as Kentucky, Tennessee, Virginia, Pennsylvania, etc.," said Charlene Hoff, one of the staff members at the genealogy library. "The library subscribes to Ancestry.com, which has a wealth of information and is accessible by subscription only. We have three public computers for the patrons to use."

In addition, staff members have gone through microfilm and printed out obituaries and other announcements and put them in books by category and year to make research a little less daunting for the patrons. Hoff said that those who visit the library have commented that they like the setup and feel that it is well organized and easy to use. The wireless Internet setup also allows folks to bring their laptops and network with other online facilities.

Hoff continued:

> *They also like the fact that the staff at the Genealogy and History House is on hand to assist the patrons when help is needed. In fact, the library also has classes to help people begin their search, and it's not surprising that the library has about 270 patrons a month. Everyone has a story*

to tell, and the people who grew up here in town can tell some interesting stories about how things used to be. We had one gentleman who has become very interested in the buildings on the square, the old houses, the furniture manufacturers, etc...and comes in to do research."

ARCHITECTURE

Another nod to the past is the historical architecture in and around Shelby County. Though styles of architecture have changed over time based on the trend of the moment, Shelby County has a diverse amount of architectural styles. Downtown Shelbyville is a wonderful representation of this, as the buildings reflect the changing times from Gothic Revival (1830–60) to Art Moderne (1930–50). Private homes and commercial buildings all showcase some of the unique trends in building over the decades.

Visitors to Shelbyville can take a walking tour and see some of the more noted structures around town, including the IOOF Building at 26 Public Square. Built in 1852, it was the building the Odd Fellows and the Masons used as a meeting hall. After these fraternal organizations left the building, a major overhaul was conducted in 1883, offering an eclectic mixture of styles

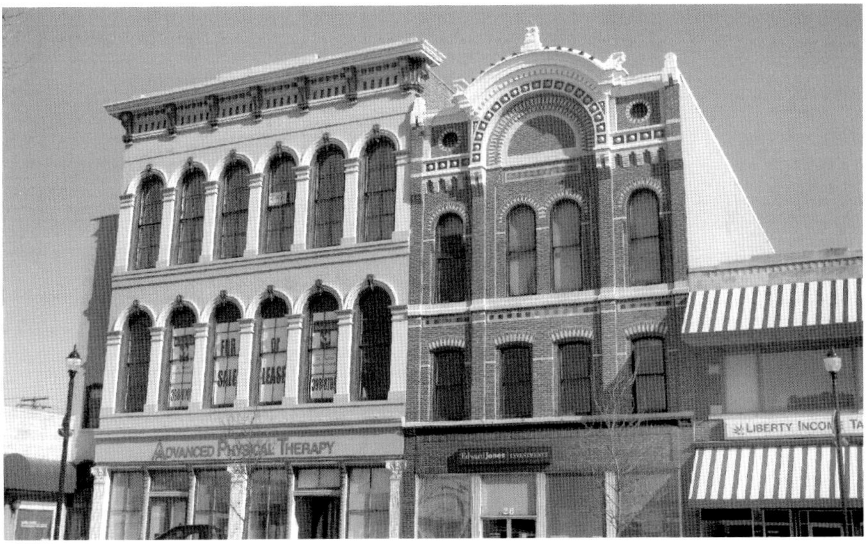

The IOOF building on the Public Square was a lodge building as well as a storefront. It has been remodeled over the years and possesses Italianate and Romanesque influences. *Author's private collection.*

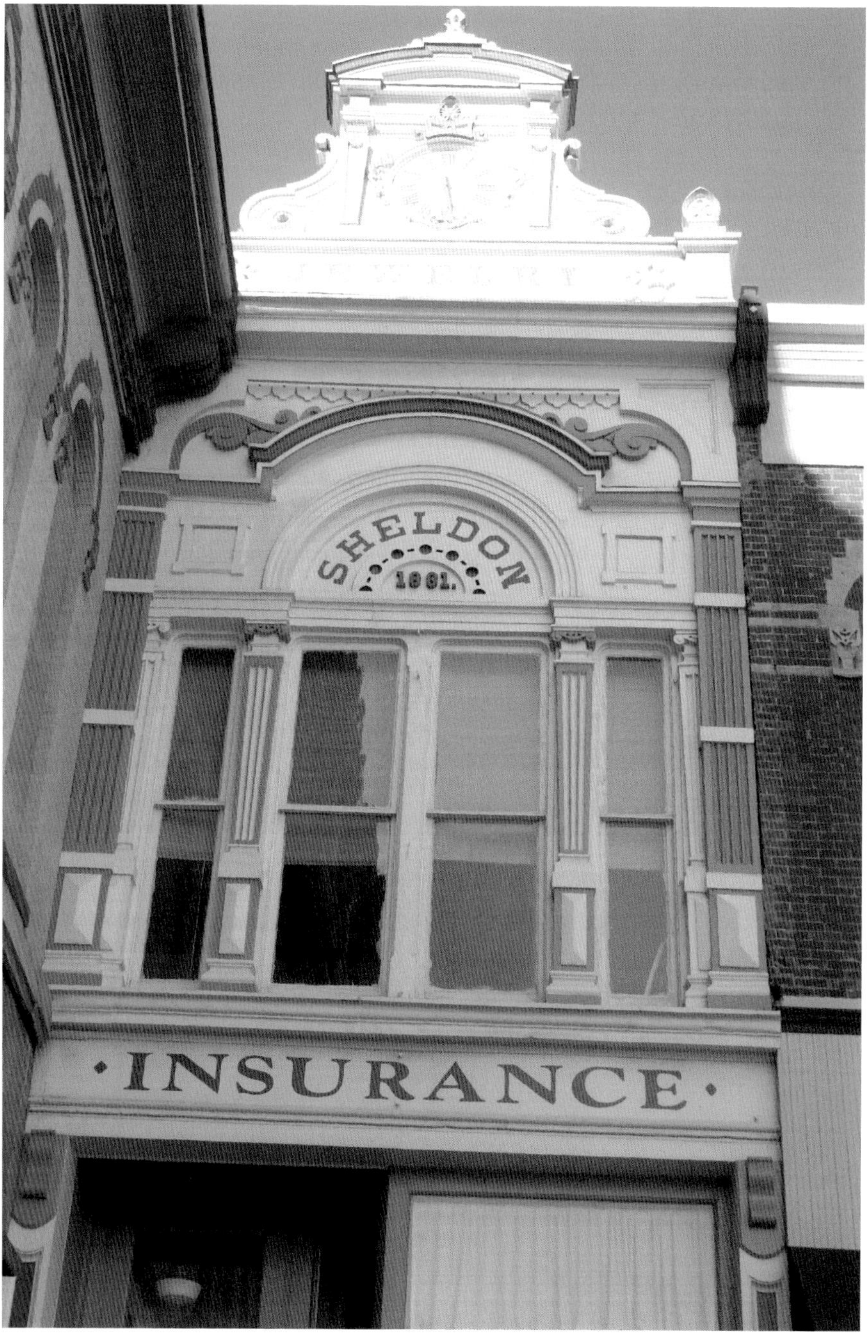

The Sheldon Building is today an insurance agency, but years ago, it was a jewelry store. The clock tower is the crowning glory of this building. *Author's private collection.*

reminiscent of Italianate and Romanesque architecture that may be seen on the façade.

When Frank Sheldon moved to Shelby County in 1875, he opened a jewelry store on the Public Square, where he owned and operated his shop until 1919. This Italianate building boasts a cast-iron front and plenty of detailing. The most impressive feature of the building, of course, is the Italian Baroque cupola that houses a huge clock for passersby to consult. Though it is an insurance agency now, the name Sheldon is still prominently featured on the building as a reminder of the Adrian, Michigan native who contributed a lot to the community.

Today, the Knights of Pythias Building, built in 1901, is a children's clothing store, but when it was constructed, it was the only building on the

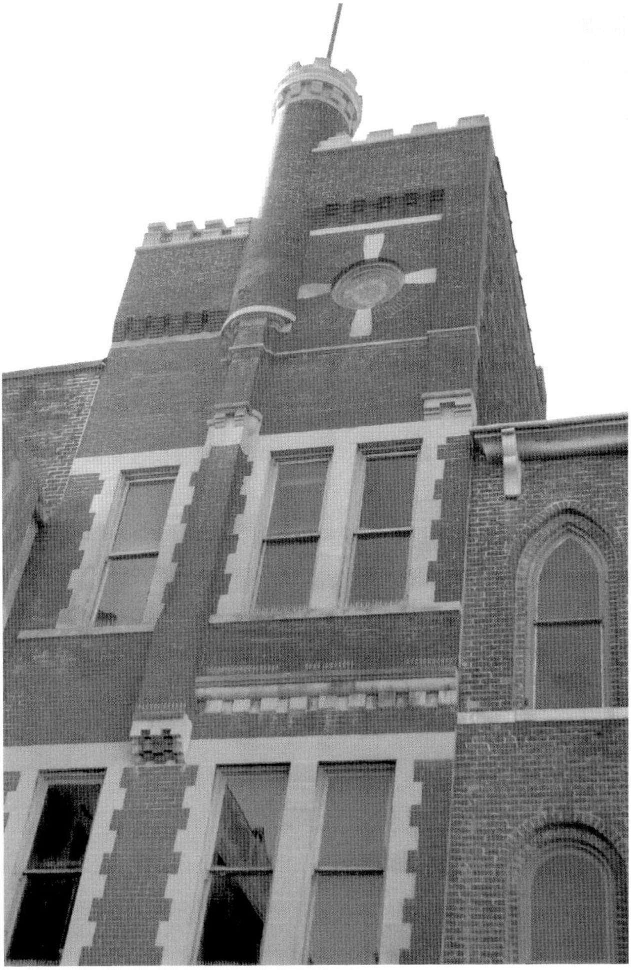

The Knights of Pythias building on the Public Square looks narrow from the street but is actually quite large. It was built in the medieval castle style. *Author's private collection.*

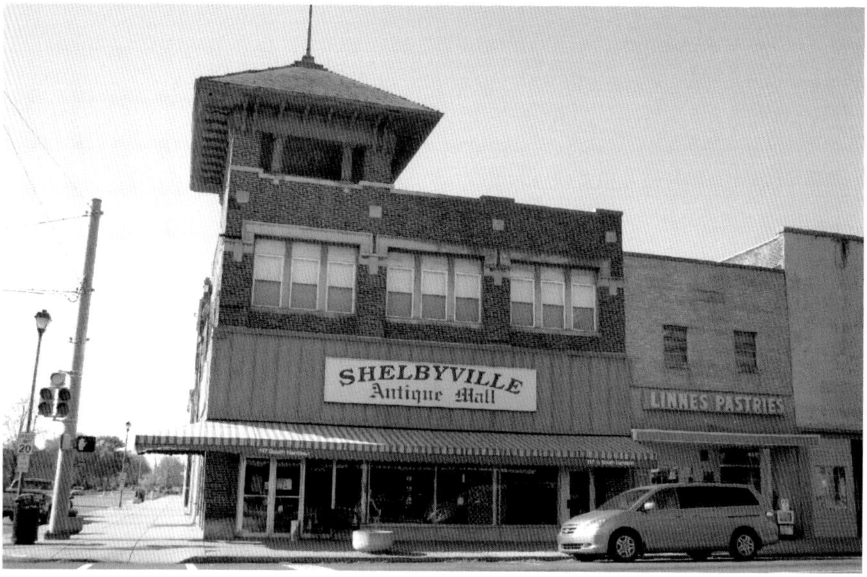

The Alhambra Theatre building was once the place to be for silent movies. The building has been remodeled over the years and is currently an antique store. *Author's private collection.*

Public Square that reflected a medieval castle style. According to the walking tour brochure, "The narrow façade disguises the fact that the Knights of Pythias Building is one of the largest on the square. Most of the structure is hidden behind others." The upper floors of Lodge No. 129 offered the organization plenty of meeting space, while the ground floor was leased to people with business interests.

Another building that is a shadow of its original use is the Alhambra Theatre building at 119 South Harrison Street. Constructed in 1913, the structure was built by Frank Rembusch, a manufacturer of motion picture screens. The theatre converted to the "talkies" in 1929, and over the years, Rembusch would own a number of theatres throughout Indiana and Illinois. He went on to become the president of the Motion Picture Exhibitors of America, but the theatre building, which boasts an Arts and Crafts feel, was repurposed for retail ventures. The storefronts have all been converted over the years, but the second floor retains its Arts and Crafts flavor.

"The most striking stylistic feature is the corner tower. The tower's roof has a wide overhanging eave supported by delicate brackets," according to the tour brochure.

Houses of worship in Shelby County often reflect a quaint prairie-style Gothic Revival architecture, which focus on vertical lines and a pointed arch. This style set the buildings apart from their residential counterparts, which were heavily influenced by the Queen Anne movement from 1880 to 1910. Some of the grander homes feature Italianate styles that were popular during the Victorian era, but others showcase an eclectic or prairie style.

For a large example of the Queen Anne style, visitors can see the C.H. Campbell House at 203 West Washington Street. Built in 1903, Campbell's home is very large and is a great example of late Queen Anne architecture. The walking tour's brochure describes the home as a "complex form with a number of Queen Anne hallmarks including a wrap-around porch, projecting bays, Tudor style chimney, and complex roof form." The home also possesses some Colonial Revival stylings as well, but overall the house was created in order to reflect the grandness of the owner of what was supposedly the largest hall furniture manufacturer in the world.

Even the Art Deco movement is represented in Shelby County. Experiencing its success thanks to the 1925 Exposition in Paris, Art Deco is at its heart a modernization of other styles. Art Deco features bold geometric influences and vertical emphasis. Ornamentation is usually held to the lower part of the structure, as well. The Methodist Building at 20 Public Square is a great example of this fun architectural trend.

"In 1917, the First Methodist Church took an option on the northwest corner of Washington and Harrison Streets, and 11 years later constructed an office building," reads the brochure. Not long after, the five-story building became known as the only skyscraper in the city. Today, it stands as a beautiful example of Art Deco style with the ground floor being defined while the upper floors are uniform and simple. The brochure notes that the stone cornice features geometric forms and a sundial.

Modern Conveniences

Shelby County has moved with the times, bringing to the region any number of manufacturing campuses and industries. From GE to Coca-Cola, from the Knauf insulation plant to Klostermann Bakeries, Shelby County has seen many companies come and go over the years.

Two of the more recent developments that have provided a great advantage to the community were the building of Indiana Downs Race Track and Indiana Live Casino! Indiana Downs is the place to go for excellence in food, fun and, of course, live horse racing. Located just off I-74, Indiana Downs

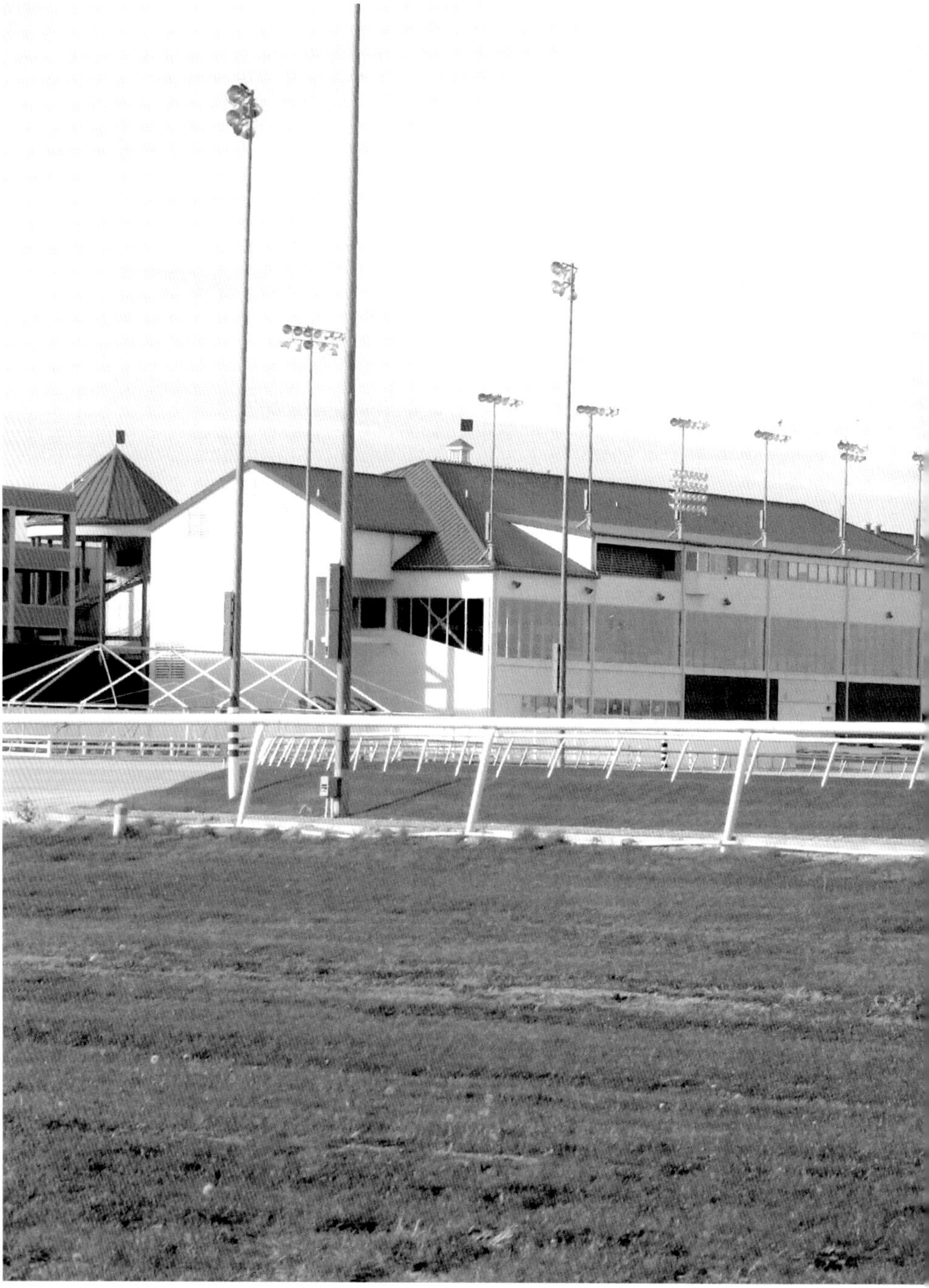

Indiana Downs racetrack has been a boon for the community economically and features a family-friendly atmosphere. Guests enjoy live races as well as off-track betting in the clubhouse. *Author's private collection.*

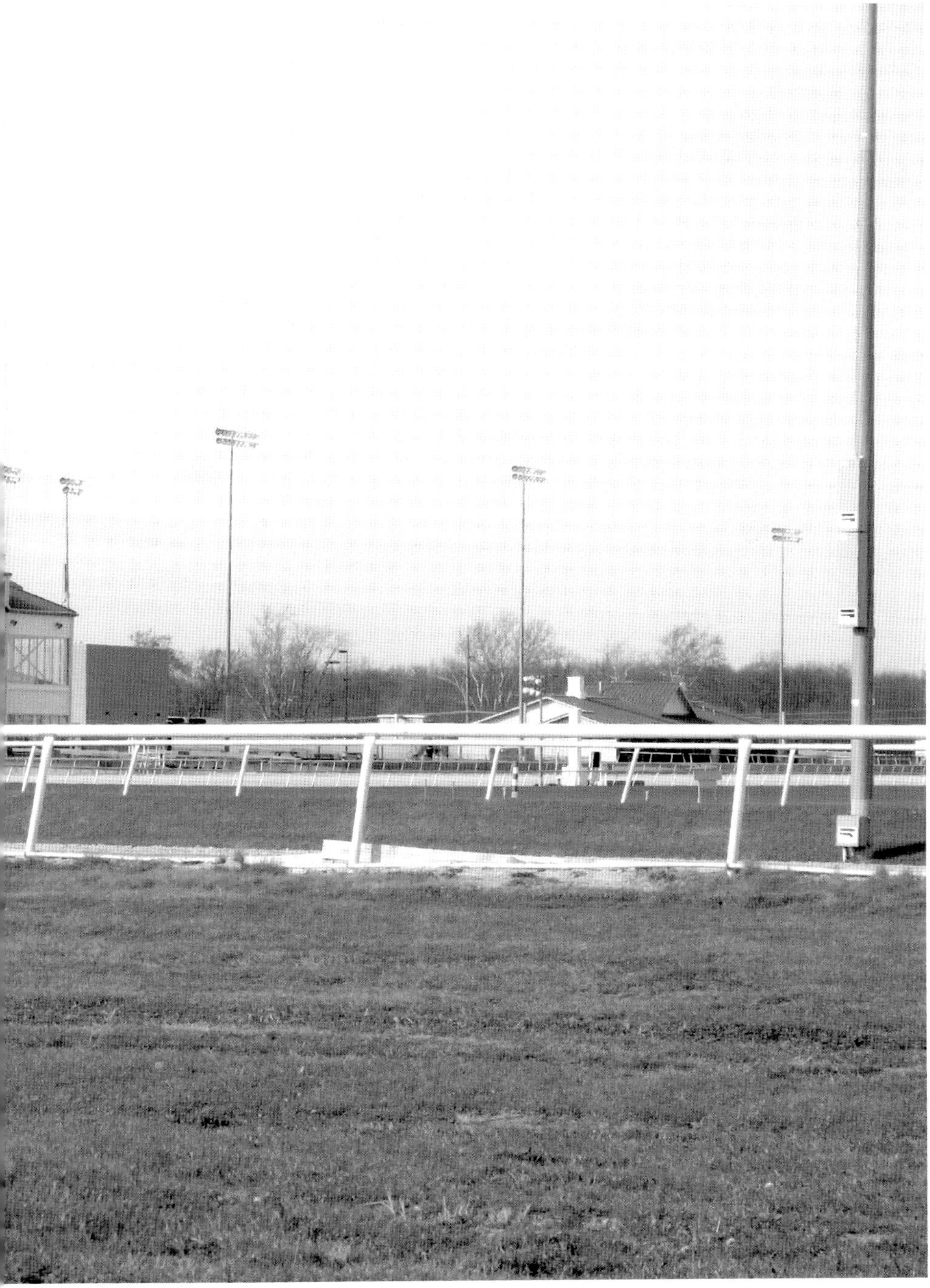

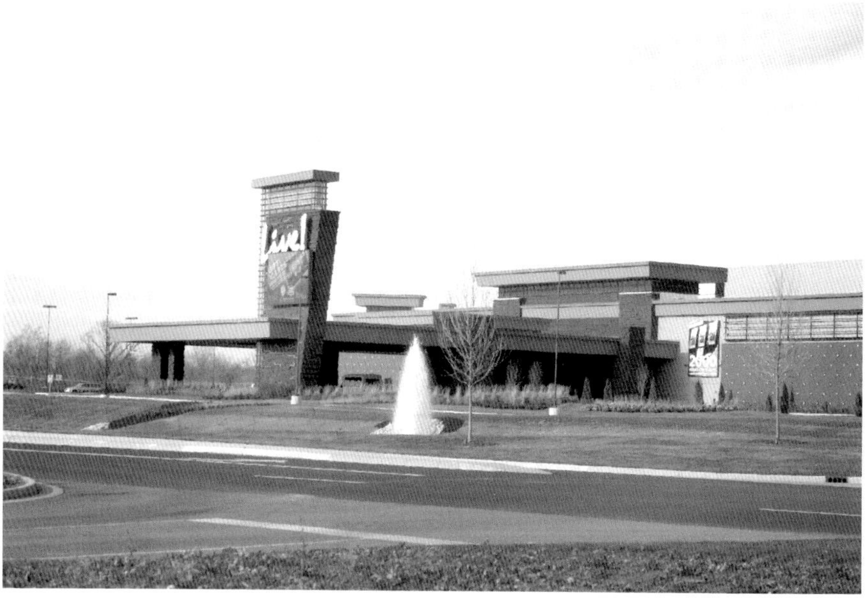

Indiana Live Casino! opened in 2008 and has been voted one of the best casinos in the Midwest. Open twenty-four hours a day, this place is always packed. *Author's private collection.*

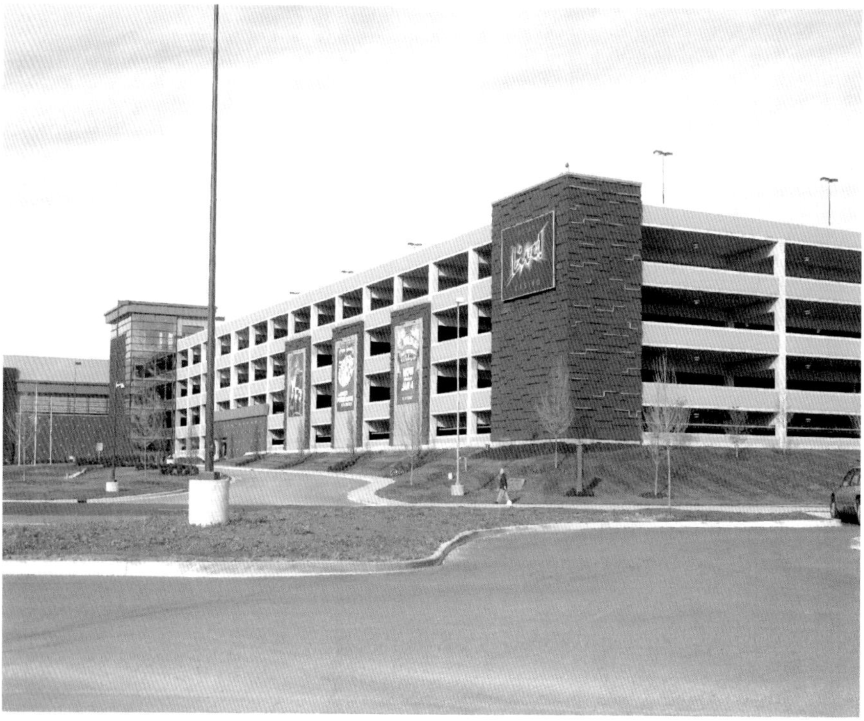

is a beautiful, family-friendly facility that features a beautiful clubhouse, restaurant, bar, arcade and plenty of other amenities for its guests.

Indiana Downs opened in 2002 with an indoor seating capacity of about three thousand situated on a two-hundred-acre track. According to the track's website, construction costs of the facility were a staggering $35 million. The track has facilities that can be rented for business entertaining, track-side suites and a gift shop with a variety of items to choose from.

When Indiana Live Casino! opened, it was as if a little touch of Vegas came to town. Initially, it was a 70,000-square-foot structure, completed within five months and opening in July 2008, but by March 2009, the new 233,000-square-foot facility had opened, and it is the largest land-based casino in the Midwest.

The facility has been honored with a number of accolades, including the Best Slots, Best Customer Service and Best Buffet, according to *Southern Gaming & Destinations Magazine*. The casino and racetrack contribute significantly to the community through charitable initiatives, the creation of jobs and other special promotions designed to return benefits to the area.

"The Indiana Live Casino! family believes it is extremely important to be involved in the community, and selected to back the Marine Corps Toys for Tots program to support deserving children, and the overall military initiative," said Mark Hemmerle, general manager of Indiana Live Casino! The casino also supports the American Red Cross, donating thousands of dollars to aid flood victims and others in the Indiana area who have suffered the effects of natural disasters.

The Trains Keep Rollin'

Shelby County is still a railroad community, with CSX Transportation, Inc. serving as the main rail line through the county. CSX's roots date back to 1828 with the birth of the B&O Railroad. From 1830 to 1860, a number of lines were constructed up and down the East Coast. Railroads were particularly important during the Civil War for the transport of men and supplies, and for this reason, they were often a target of the warring armies.

According to the CSX website, in 1868, when the states were reunited, Virginia and West Virginia legislatures provided for the completion of lines from Chesapeake Bay to the Ohio River. The Virginia Central Railroad was renamed the Chesapeake and Ohio Railroad (C&O) as the company assumed the rights, interests and privileges of the Covington and Ohio Railroad. The C&O would be reorganized by 1878 and renamed the Chesapeake and Ohio Railway.

Throughout the first part of the twentieth century, America's rail lines peaked with an impressive 254,000 track miles, but more and more lines would consolidate in an effort to streamline operations. The name CSX emerged in 1980 when the Chessie System and the Seaboard Coast Line Industries, Inc. (two lines created by the merging of other small railways) consolidated, setting the stage for today's strong railroad foundation in Shelby County.

Between 1997 and 1999, CSX was able to partner with Norfolk Southern for Conrail's operations, gaining 3,200 miles of track and offering the company more of a chance to improve rail service. In March 2007, CSX became the first company in the transportation industry to join the U.S. Environmental Protection Agency's Climate Leaders Program. On an average day, CSX operates 1,200 trains and transports 20,000 carloads of products and raw material, making its commitment to cleaner air an important component to its daily operations.

According to a company press release:

> *Since 2000, CSXT has invested more than $1 billion to upgrade its locomotive fleet with technology that reduces both fuel consumption and air pollutant emissions. Through these efforts, the company has improved its fuel efficiency by approximately 90 percent since 1980. By the end of 2009, 1,200 CSXT locomotives will be upgraded to further reduce emissions and lower fuel consumption by nearly 10 million gallons.*

KNAUF INSULATION

The Knauf Company has been a boon to Shelby County since 1978, when the Knauf family purchased a fiberglass production facility in Shelbyville. A family company that was started in 1932 by Karl and Dr. Alfons N. Knauf, it is a multinational producer of building materials and construction systems. Knauf began in gypsum processing in Germany but eventually became a company that diversified into fields such as plasterboard, screeds, glasswool, rock mineral wool and wood wool cement insulation, in addition to various building products. In 1990, the company opened its third North American plant, which manufactures pipe insulation.

In 2005, the company broke ground to begin a $200 million–plus renovation of the original Shelbyville plant, which was completed in 2008 and included the addition of square footage to the building, as well as state-of-the-art computer technology geared to improving product quality.

According to the company's press release, the expansion included 373,000 square feet of warehousing and roughly 300,000 square feet of production facilities. Along with Knauf's residential lines, the plant produces commercial and industrial insulation products, including duct and equipment insulations, and uncured products, as well as light-density building insulations. The plant now boasts more than double the production capacity using a fully automated manufacturing process complete with technology upgrades that provide greater control of product quality. A single networked system was created by coupling controlled manufacturing processes with Programmable Logic Controllers (PLCs), instruments that control the Human Machine Interface (HMI) and other high-tech improvements.

"Our advanced computer control technology provides continuous feedback during every step of the production process. Real-time process adjustments are made based on that feedback," says Jon Pereira, senior vice-president of operations at Knauf. "This state-of-the-art technology allows the plant to consistently produce more of the same high-quality products Knauf is known for while using much less energy."

With expansions designed to keep Knauf moving forward, as well as a significant amount of people in the region employed, Knauf is committed to its missions and value statement, which says that it strives to do "good things for the communities in which we work as well as for the environment in which we live. We work hard, but we enjoy doing it. Taking pride and having pleasure in our work is part of who we are and what makes us get out of bed in the morning."

Klosterman Bakery

Located in Morristown, Klosterman Baking Company, Inc. is one of the largest family-owned bakeries in the Midwest. Specializing in hearth breads, rolls and a variety of other baked goods for restaurants and other institutions, the secret to Klosterman's success has been passed through the generations for more than one hundred years.

Kim Klosterman wrote on the company blog:

> *Our family arrived in Cincinnati more than a century ago, armed with prized family recipes. Basic to our trade at the time was the quality of the dough, made the old-fashioned way, using only the finest ingredients. These quality standards remain in our family business today—but back then, products were sold door to door from a horse-drawn wagon. Today, our family business continues to grow, and we're proud to say, it has become one of the largest family-owned bakeries in the Midwest. These successes have come from listening to you, our consumers, and ensuring we continue to bake the products you want, and can feel good about serving your family. I personally know that you take a great deal of pride in the products you put on your family's meal tables.*

Still a Farming Community

At its core, Shelby County remains a quiet farming community with rich histories of families who have tilled the land for generations. In 1991, the Buschkoetter family moved to Shelby County in order to live in a 140-year-old farmhouse with nine acres of land. The family farm today has a smokehouse, barn, corncrib, garage and chicken coop. While some of the buildings are now used for storage, the family still raises rabbits, chickens, turkeys and guineas.

"As a family, we love living in the country and learning about the history of the buildings surrounding us. The house down the street is the original log cabin where Balser lived from *Bears of Blue River*. It is always neat to drive through the town circle, and I often did when I was in high school, but we considered it 'the strip.' We all had our spots where we would sit and visit with other friends," said Alicia Buschkoetter, a sixth-grade teacher at Little Flower Catholic School in Indianapolis. "I still enjoy driving through the circle when I come home for church at St. Vincent's, helping mom with her sorority, and visiting high school friends who lived in Shelbyville. The Shelby County fair was also an attraction that I still come home for. I enjoyed participating in 4-H for four years and so did my brothers. Now they are consumed with Boy Scouts and the St. Joseph's Parish. I also went to the Bears of Blue River Festival around the circle. Shelbyville is just like a family."

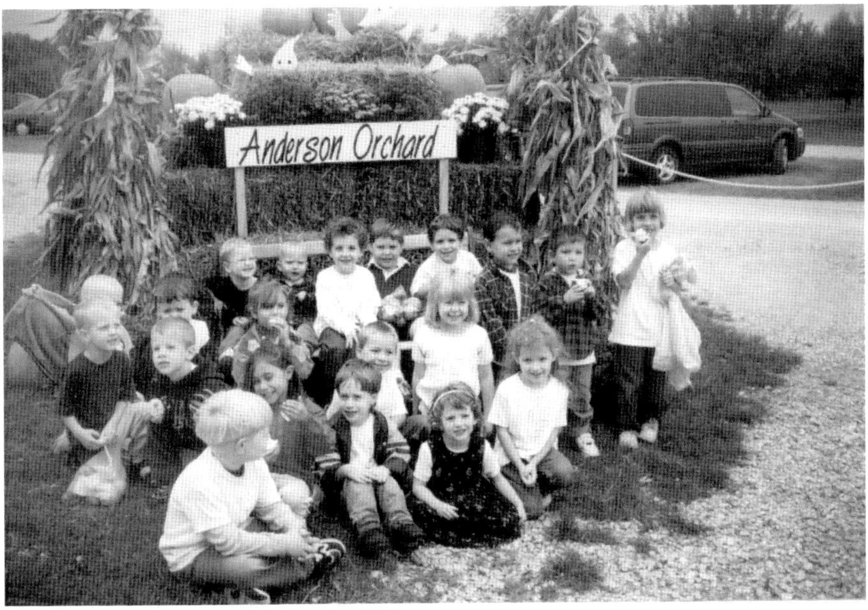

Students from Little Flower Catholic Grade School in Indianapolis enjoy a field trip to Anderson Orchard in Fairland. *Author's private collection.*

Other entities include the Anderson Orchard. Since the 1930s, Anderson Orchard in Pleasant View has been a staple for those who want to buy fresh apples from local markets or experience the thrill of picking their own.

In 1994, Bud and Gloria Hopkins purchased the orchard, which continues to draw crowds annually, from school groups to local residents who want to taste and pick from over eighteen varieties of apples. In addition, Anderson specializes in a variety of apple products such as preserves, apple butter, fresh produce, cider, caramel apples, candles and baked goods. "Our goal is to make your trip to the orchard one that keeps you coming back," says the orchard website. "We hope you will share your experience with family and friends."

In order to keep the agricultural heritage alive and inspire a new generation of growers, Anderson offers field trips for school groups to enable children to experience a country setting while learning about how apples grow. It is all part of how Shelby County growers continue the traditions that helped establish the county so long ago.

CONCLUSION

It feels as though a lifetime has passed since I began this book. In the months it took to gather the photos and organize the text, I lost a lot of sleep, moved and worried consistently that I was not doing justice to all that is Shelby County. During a recent conversation with Grover Museum director Candace Miller, she recognized my anxiety and assured me that the community would be excited by the prospective volume that was not a tome but rather a short celebration of the rich Shelby County history that would offer a peek into the past. She also thought it would be a wonderful starting place for Shelby County students to learn something of local history while inspiring them to visit historical venues and libraries to learn more. I know I learned a lot, so maybe they will too.

The funny thing about writing a book is that no matter how I map it out, at some point, it usually takes on a life of its own, and I am simply along for the ride. This book was like that as well. During the early days of research, I was sitting in the Blue Bird Restaurant in Morristown listening to my great-aunts as they started discussing the POW camp and the prisoners as though they were talking about the weather. I scrambled for a pen and a piece of paper to catch their thoughts, musing at the fact that "lunch" suddenly had become an interview session.

In my opinion, this is the best way to learn about history: listening to the people and their experiences. I know I certainly learn a lot more from hearing people tell me about personal experiences than I ever did memorizing dates, facts and minutiae that seemed to be the core of my high school history texts. Through the writing of this book, I met people who knew my family members and were quick to share stories that made my day and made this book become very personal to me.

As I finish this book, I am pleased to say that Shelby County has a lot going for it, and I hope that throughout the twenty-first century, the county continues to make its mark in a big way. I am very proud that it is one of my neighboring counties and that it is an area that contributes a lot to the central Indiana region. Shelby County deserves a lot of credit and doesn't always get the opportunity to take a lot of bows.

While traveling home from Shelbyville one November afternoon, I saw the farm equipment out harvesting the corn that would be used for seed next spring, as well as fodder for animals and foodstuff for humans. Perhaps a little of it is going to biofuel research as well, but it occurred to me that without the hardworking farmers of areas like Shelby County, there would be no food on our plates. Without major employers such as the Intelliplex industrial technology park, Klosterman and Indiana Live Casino!, there would be more Hoosiers out of jobs, and I applaud the investors who saw the potential in Shelby County and had the vision to turn the community into a destination for visitors and new residents from all over the Midwest.

I am also thrilled with the amount of small businesses in and around the county. These are owned and operated by the new local "visionaries" who believe that Shelby County is the place where they can realize their American dream, and I encourage everyone who reads this book to shop local and buy local. Truly, this is the way to build community and support one another.

The other thing I love about Shelby County is the feeling of nostalgia when I visit my family members in Morristown or drive through London and Boggstown. These are communities that are still alive despite their age and in the face of a world that moves at the speed of light. In my opinion, we need communities like this, and it is important that those who live and work in small towns put in the sweat equity in order to keep these burgs viable. What a shame it would be if all we had left were old picture postcards and a few memories. I am beyond blessed when I am able to take my children to the Kopper Kettle and let them see the gardens I enjoyed as a little girl or attend Derby Days so they can make a few memories of their own as they catch candy thrown from parade riders and cheer for the fastest racer.

While much has been written about the early days of Shelby County, I encourage residents to write their own stories, young and young at heart alike. We must preserve the personal history that exists in this community in order to pay homage to the past and set the stage for a very exciting future.

BIBLIOGRAPHY

Boggstown Cabaret. www.boggstown.com.

Decker, Jeff. "Fast Racers and Fast Friendships." *Indianapolis Star*, n.d.

Hicks, Jim. "Marjorie Main." http://www.geocities.com/gimcrack.geo/MarjorieMain.html. No longer available.

"The History of London and Brookfield." Booklet, n.d.

Kopper Kettle. www.KopperKettle.com.

Krokos, Mike. "History, Culture at Heart of Annual Italian POW Chapel Reunion." *The Criterion*, August 28, 2009, 16.

Major Hospital. "History of Major Hospital." http://www.majorhospital.com/newsite/Infodesk/AboutUs/history.php.

McDaniel, Carol. "Derby Day Festivities Keep Growing." *Indianapolis Star*, n.d.

McFadden, Marian. *Biography of a Town: Shelbyville, Indiana 1822–1962*. Shelbyville, IN: Tippicanoe Press, Inc., 1968.

Rock, Florence. *Memoirs of Mrs. Florence Johnson Rock and Historical Sketches*. Morristown, IN: 1946.

Town of Edinburgh. www.edinburgh.in.us.

Wikipedia. "Edna Parker." http://en.wikipedia.org/wiki/Edna_Parker.

———. "James Pierce." http://en.wikipedia.org/wiki/James_Pierce.

———. "Marjorie Main." http://en.wikipedia.org/wiki/Marjorie_Main.

———. "Sandy Allen." http://en.wikipedia.org/wiki/Sandy_Allen.

———."Thomas Hendricks." http://en.wikipedia.org/wiki/Thomas_Hendricks.

———. "William Garrett." http://en.wikipedia.org/wiki/Bill_Garrett_(basketball).

Wolf, Buck. "A Big Goodbye to Sandy Allen, World's Tallest Woman." Buck's Weird News Blog. http://weirdnews.about.com/b/2008/08/14/a-big-goodby-to-sandy-allen-worlds-tallest-woman.htm. August 14, 2008.

Women's Society of Christian Service. *Hoosier Recipes from Fairland Kitchens*. N.p.: Fairland Methodist Church, 1952.

Young, Julie. "11-year-old Middle-Schooler Travels with a Fast Crowd." *Indianapolis Star*, n.d.

ABOUT THE AUTHOR

Julie Young is a freelance writer and author from the Indianapolis area who has written for a number of local, regional and national publications, including the *Indianapolis Star*, the *Indianapolis Monthly*, *Indianapolis House & Home*, *AAA Home & Away*, *Today's Catholic Teacher Magazine* and CNN.com. In 2000, she appeared on the *Oprah Winfrey Show*. Her first book, *A Belief in Providence: A Life of Saint Theodora Guerin*, was a 2008 finalist in the Best Books in Indy competition. She is also the author of *Images of America: Historic Irvington* and *Eastside Indianapolis: A Brief History*. For more information, please visit www.julieyoungfreelance.com.